BEETHOVEN

by

DONALD FRANCIS TOVEY

*Sometime Reid Professor of Music in the
University of Edinburgh*

With an Editorial Preface by

HUBERT J. FOSS

OXFORD UNIVERSITY PRESS

London   Oxford   New York

Oxford University Press

LONDON OXFORD NEW YORK

GLASGOW TORONTO MELBOURNE WELLINGTON

CAPE TOWN IBADAN NAIROBI DAR ES SALAAM LUSAKA ADDIS ABABA

DELHI BOMBAY CALCUTTA MADRAS KARACHI LAHORE DACCA

KUALA LUMPUR SINGAPORE HONG KONG TOKYO

ISBN 0 19 284007 x

First published by Oxford University
Press, London, 1944

First issued as an Oxford University Press paperback,
1965; reprinted 1971 and 1973

For copyright reasons this book may not be
issued on loan or otherwise except in its
original soft cover

Printed in Great Britain by
Redwood Press Limited
Trowbridge, Wiltshire

EDITORIAL PREFACE

THE idea of writing a book about Beethoven occupied Donald Francis Tovey's thoughts, or the back of his mind, for the last twenty-eight years of his life. It was proposed to him in 1912, and again after the last war in about 1920. In 1936 he dictated the book which occupies the following pages.

Tovey never mentioned either the project or the partial achievement of it to me. In fact, I find considerable obscurity about the motive which actuated his setting about the making of this book. He spoke to me, indeed, with great enthusiasm of Miss Marion Scott's book referred to herein on p. 3. Of other causes I can find no trace. The MS. was found among his posthumous papers, in duplicate, unfinished as it here appears. I do not even know why it was never finished. It may have been illness, it may have been other more urgent tasks, that took his mind away from the problem which was so dear to him in conversation as Beethoven's Fugues. He expressed on more than one occasion, I am informed, an intention to re-write the book—no uncommon desire of Tovey's.

But though he never completed the book (and there is only internal evidence that the unfinished chapter was the last in the plan), Tovey began to revise the typescript. He was always a corrector of his own work. Of this book he looked over the typed pages up to p. 51: the last correction in his autograph is the addition of the words 'for this' after the phrase 'our main leading cases' which occurs in the printed text on p. 12. Up to that page, the reconsiderations are numerous and fairly extensive. I give one example here, by printing the opening sentences that Tovey first dictated, and placing in brackets the words he deleted. A turn of the page will show an inquirer the final form of the sentence on p. 1.

> Beethoven is a complete artist [. It would perhaps raise vexatious controversy to call him], one of the completest [artists] that ever lived [, but at all events it would be exceedingly difficult to find a better claimant for the title. First, however, we must be sure of what we mean by a complete artist. I intend to use the term without any reference to] the artist's private or official life [, and, therefore, without any implication] that the artist has a temperament, etc.

Another, too long to quote *in extenso*, occurs on p. 6 of the typescript and p. 2 of the printed text. The printed sentence, 'and it was at the disadvantage of fisticuffs against ju-jitsu,' was an autograph addition to the original matter. In a third

and final example, the passage (on p. 2 of the printed text) from
'By all means let us revolt against "bardolatry"' to 'Sam Weller's
criticism of life' is condensed from the typescript material occupying nearly two and a half pages, or some 400 odd words—
themselves also corrected by the author before they were crossed
out.

What other revisions Donald Tovey might have made, what
his recurrent second thoughts might have been, is beyond calcula-
tion or imagination. The typescript is incomplete in another way,
that of the musical and even poetic quotations. There are spaces
left, without more hint than the text gives.

In preparing this typescript (I call it so persistently because
it was never a manuscript, except in the revisions), I have relied
firmly and confidently upon Dr. Ernest Walker, who knew Donald
Tovey's mind, from his undergraduate days, better perhaps than
any one else. Where he and I have been absolutely clear about
Tovey's intentions I have inserted musical examples, and indeed
even in one or two other places where Tovey had planned no
illuminating quotation. In other places, minor alterations to the
text have been made—far less in quantity than Tovey himself
made in the first pages of the typescript, and not one of a kind
that could alter his meaning. Repetitions have been retained,
and even minor slacknesses of prose style, in order to present the
book in as nearly as possible its original form. The proofs have
been independently read by Mr. Robert C. Trevelyan. I have
elsewhere explained that Tovey needed his books to be made for
him. This text has suffered, I can assert, less revision than it
would have suffered in Tovey's lifetime.

Thanks are due to Dr. Walker and Mr. Trevelyan for their
assistance and guidance, and also to Lady Tovey for the opportunity and permission to print this book. Every Toveyan is also
indebted, both here and elsewhere, to Dr. Mary Grierson for her
labours and for her knowledge of 'the Professor's mind'.

1944   HUBERT J. FOSS

CONTENTS

THE MATERIALS OF BEETHOVEN'S LANGUAGE

BEETHOVEN is a complete artist. If the term is rightly understood, he is one of the completest that ever lived. I intend to use the term without pedantic scruples as to technical details. And, while admitting that 'the style is the man', I refuse to involve the reader in vulgar entanglements between the art and the artist's private or official life. Beethoven was of all men the last to tolerate the belief that the artist has a temperament which sets him above the standards of ordinary citizenship, or excuses his failure to reach them. Whatever his sins may have been (and on this subject the evidence is doubtful), he was eminently a man who held himself responsible. Joachim once remarked of a clever French musical critic that 'this Parisian shows no sense for the great penitent that there was in Beethoven'. Beethoven was far too busy to torment himself, but Joachim was profoundly right about his penitence. It was a quality that was, if possible, more out of fashion in Beethoven's time than it is now. But it will always be inseparable from responsibility so long as human beings have ideals and fail to reach them. I do not know if a modern teacher of autosuggestion could have shortened John Bunyan's agonies and brought him sooner to his land of Beulah; I am quite certain that no modern psychologist could have found anything more to shake in Beethoven than he could in Browning, or in any other person who has made up his mind about his responsibilities.

To study the lives of great artists is often a positive hindrance to the understanding of their works; for it is usually the study of what they have not mastered, and thus it undermines their authority in the things which they have mastered. To undermine that authority is an injury much more serious than any merely professional technicality. Even if the works of art show characteristics closely resembling the faults of the author, we have always to remember that the business of the work of art is to be itself, whereas neither the science of ethics nor the structure of society can thrive for long on the denial that it is the duty of a man to improve himself. A sense of duty imposed upon a work of art from without is artistic insincerity. Whatever goes into the work of art must belong to it. We must not impute it as a defect in Wagner's aesthetic system that his music dramas tend to glorify irresponsibility, or at all events to remove from his heroes and heroines, even by means as crude as magic potions, every hindrance to the attainments of their desires. We have outgrown the critical fallacy which misuses Matthew Arnold's definition of poetry as a 'criticism of life'. Matthew Arnold was more careful about his use of it than some later writers who have used his words as evidence against him. But we have been less ready to outgrow the crude reaction which positively demands that a work of art should shock rather than instruct. We have now come to see that a reverence for the music dramas of Wagner is quite compatible with a dislike for the Saxon (I will not say Anglo-Saxon) traits by which Wagner the man, like the patriots in *The Critic*, was apt to pray to his gods to prosper his ends and sanctify the means he used to gain them. But we have been slower to attain, even if we have yet attained, the realization that Beethoven does not become an inartistic preacher because of the fact that his sense of responsibility is an essential part of his musical style. To put the matter in unfashionable terms, Beethoven's music is edifying. There is nothing inartistic in that. The anti-romantic revolt against Beethoven in the first quarter of this century was too manifestly ill-bred and silly to mean much, and it was at the disadvantage of fisticuffs against ju-jitsu. Beethoven's sense of duty was to preach; and, whatever may be found in commentaries on Beethoven, there is in his own works even less of a doctrine from which revolt is possible than there is in Shakespeare's. By all means let us revolt against 'bardolatry'; but let us avoid the literal-minded errors of the preacher who has no use for the poet, even though the preacher be Plato or Bernard Shaw, and the poet Homer or Shakespeare.

What the poet says is not evidence in a court of law. In the leading case of *Bardell* v. *Pickwick*, Stareleigh J. forbade the witness Weller to quote what the soldier said. But though what the soldier said was not evidence, it was a good illustration of Sam Weller's criticism of life. What I hope to bring out in the course of this book is the fact that Beethoven's psychology, to use the popular jargon of to-day, is always right. His music is, in fact, a supremely masterly and hopeful criticism of life. The difficulties and dangers of demonstrating this arise mainly from the fact that music can be described only in terms of music. But I have the less excuse for shirking the task, because evidence has already reached me that readers who cannot read musical notation have wrestled not unsuccessfully with essays in which I have not avoided technicalities. In these days of broadcasting and gramophone records, readers will differ widely about what they find too technical, and I am frankly more troubled by the difficulties of readers who have some little text-book knowledge than by those of the really naïve listener. It would take too much space if I were to give warning of the approach of every piece of argument which may be tiresome to some readers. Each person must satisfy his own curiosity. None of the topics that I shall discuss will fail at one time or another to arouse the curiosity of non-professional music-lovers, and my last word in defence of my present policy is that, though I cannot forbid the use of this book by degree-students, I have not designed it as a text-book for examinations.

Recently two books on Beethoven have saved me from the trouble of attempting either a new biography of Beethoven or a philosophic account of his relation to his age. The philosophy of Beethoven's style has been discussed with great insight by Mr. J. W. N. Sullivan,[1] and his biography has been handled with powers of vivid narrative and a charity akin to Beethoven's own by Miss Marion Scott,[2] who has also dealt with the music in a manner which it would be difficult to over-praise. It is only in respect of the music that I am tempted to add anything to the contents of these admirable works, or even to record my disagreement with the writers on details here and there. But the task of dealing with the music as music is more than enough for me; and, even now that an intelligent interest in music is more widely distributed than the music-lovers of last century could ever have dreamt of as possible, there is crying need for a clearer understanding of the nature of music itself. And by this I do not mean the philosophic subject which Mr. Sullivan discusses under that title, but the humble and professional facts of rhythm, melody, counterpoint, harmony, and tonality. Some readers are perhaps already alarmed by this list, but I am confident that in everything I have to say on these subjects the reader will find that I shall relieve the strain upon his conscience that has been caused by well-meaning professional mystifications and confusions.

So let us boldly begin with tonality, a subject which most of my professional friends believe to be beyond the comprehension of anybody but a trained musician. On rhythm we need not, for the moment, be elaborate. In music, it is, of course, the organization of sounds in respect of time. Critics of architecture, painting, and sculpture extend it by metaphor to the organization of curves and patterns. But I shall not deal with metaphors until the difficulty of the subject compels me.

Melody is not so simple a concept as people are apt to think. Strictly speaking, it should mean no more than the organization of successive musical sounds in respect of pitch, not excluding the extreme case of monotone. But, if the sounds are successive, it is impossible to organize them without rhythm; and it is a mistake to suppose that rhythm ceases to be organized when it is set free from certain restrictions, as in the case of recitative.

Harmony, in classical music, is the organization of simultaneous

[1] *Beethoven—his spiritual development.* By J. W. N. Sullivan. Cape.
[2] *Beethoven.* By Marion M. Scott. (The Master Musicians.) Dent.

musical sounds of different pitch. It is thus inseparable from
melody and rhythm. Before long we shall find that it is really
inseparable from counterpoint. (In ancient Greek music 'harmony' meant the melodic organization of scales: the simultaneous
combination of sounds was not developed beyond inevitable
rudiments.)

Tonality comprises the larger aspects of harmony, and becomes
an inseparable function of musical form. It will be my object
to convince the most general reader that, ever since he became
fond of music at all, he has enjoyed tonality whether he knew it
or not, just as Molière's *Bourgeois Gentilhomme*, Monsieur Jourdain, found that he had been talking prose all his life without
knowing it. But tonality is extraordinarily difficult to define. I
can only describe instances of it, and show it in operation in
Beethoven's works. For many years I was troubled with the fear
that this difficulty of defining tonality constituted a fatal objection
to one of the principal articles of my musical creed; my belief
that nothing in a work of art has a real aesthetic value unless it
can reach the consciousness of the spectator or listener through
the evidence of the art alone, without the aid of technical information. Though, for example, a game such as cricket or chess
is quite highly enough organized to be called artistic, the finest
games will still remain outside the region of works of art so long
as there is any doubt whether a spectator could acquire a knowledge of their essential rules merely by watching them without
technical help. Be this as it may, I am convinced that a symphony
of Beethoven is not a game, but a thing that explains itself: having
said which, I now proceed to devote this volume to an explanation
of it which nobody but a professional musician could attempt.
There is no inconsistency in this. My professional terminology
is rigorously confined to generalizations from the behaviour of
musical compositions. The non-professional music-lover has not
had time to make my generalizations for himself; and if I give
him the benefit of my experience I shall not be spoiling a story
for him by revealing its events before he has come to them. The
only thing that we professional musicians must guard against is
the danger of confusion between knowledge that is relevant to
the understanding of works of art, and knowledge which is relevant
only to the discipline of an artist's training. This also is a legitimate object of the general reader's curiosity, and I shall make no
mystery of it; but we must keep the two kinds of knowledge
distinct. Where readers may differ about what is merely technical
and what is aesthetic, I ask for the benefit of the doubt. Personally,
I have no use for any musical principle that does not seem to me
primarily aesthetic.

THE THREE DIMENSIONS OF MUSIC

RHYTHM, melody, and harmony are the obvious three dimensions of music. They are, as we have already seen, inseparable, like the three dimensions of space, though they are not interchangeable in the same way. (Now that science has definitely recognized time as a fourth dimension, it finds something like the difficulty that confronts the musician in interchanging it with the other dimensions.)

It is important to realize that the person who naïvely professes himself fond of melody is professing a fondness for a very recent development in musical thought. If he is naïve enough, or sophisticated enough, to affect a bluntness of speech, he will say that what he likes is a tune; and by 'tune' he means (as unconsciously as Monsieur Jourdain talked prose) a highly civilized product of melody based on ideas of tonality that had not yet taken shape in the reign of Queen Elizabeth, and with a kind of four-square form that hardly became a standardized quality in music before the reign of Charles II.

Very few naïve listeners profess an interest in harmony; and I will go so far in sympathy with the majority as to assert, merely as a personal opinion, that nothing bores me more intensely than a composer with a new system of harmony. This book, however, will have failed in its object if the reader does not derive from it the conviction that Beethoven is one of the supreme masters of harmony. This unsupported statement will seem a violent paradox. A good writer has recently observed that no composer of anything like Beethoven's calibre has contributed so little to the development of harmony. At the present moment it will suffice to anticipate further discussion by saying that Beethoven's contribution to harmony is a long-range power of handling tonality and that the long-range handling of tonality is in its earlier stages downright incompatible with concentration upon new chords and new progressions. What most people mean by 'new harmonic developments' is equivalent to such features of style as George Meredith's metaphors. It is ridiculous to suppose that either the structure of a novel or its author's 'criticism of life' can be built up merely from the surface ornaments of his wit, even though every one of his epigrams should contain a profound philosophic truth.

In any case, harmony is a very much larger musical category than any harmonic theorist, classical or revolutionary, has made of it. Many readers will need warning that every member of Western civilization who has enjoyed as much as a barrel-organ has thereby acquired notions of harmony and tonality that would have been unintelligible five hundred years ago. The late Mr. Dolmetsch's recent researches into Welsh harp-music have convinced musical scholars that, with every allowance for a certain Dolmetschian optimism, some of our classical notions of harmony are profound instincts which asserted themselves in music of a much greater antiquity than has hitherto been supposed to imply any harmonic consciousness at all. Be this as it may, we must realize that our most popular notions of harmony are naïve only relatively to us, and that as actual aesthetic concepts they are anything but raw material. I shall not attempt to explain them more fully than is absolutely necessary for the purpose of removing obstacles to our understanding of Beethoven. Many of the obstacles arise from technical terms of musical form and grammar that have crept into popular currency and lost their proper meaning.

The general reader and the professional musician are equally prone to form preposterous ideas of the demands which a great piece of music makes upon the technical experience of the listener. Let us now boldly attack the most purely musical and indescribable part of our problem—the nature of tonality, and especially of Beethoven's development of it. It may not be scientific to begin with this. But it is not our task to prove scientifically that Beethoven existed or that he was a great artist. I choose tonality as my starting-point, partly in order to get over the most difficult subject first, but also because it is a subject on which the reader can learn much by experiment with a simple apparatus which in one form or another will surely be within his reach. Some of the keenest and most intelligent lovers of music have never learnt to read musical notation, and they must rely on the help they can get from listening to music in general and hearing by one means or another the illustrations given in this book. For those who can read music and who have a pianoforte in the house, a volume of Beethoven's complete Pianoforte Sonatas will be a good apparatus to begin with. The edition does not much matter, so long as it presents Beethoven's original text clearly separated from whatever editorial comment may be present. There is not space in this book for particulars of the grave corruptions that have crept into classical music through the activity of instructive editors, especially pianists, who are so much cleverer than the composer that their instructions are destructive of his text. It is probable that where there is a pianoforte and a buyer of this book there will already be a volume of Beethoven's Pianoforte Sonatas. Miniature scores of all except a very few of Beethoven's works are available at moderate prices for each individual score, though your shillings soon become pounds when you begin to collect scores in earnest. But if you can read musical notation at all you will soon find that orchestral scores become intelligible if you practise not only following from the score while the music is heard at a concert or by wireless or gramophone, but also if, while the experience is fresh, you try to recapture from the look of the page something like the quality as well as the meaning of the sound. It is a mistake to be too analytical in this practice.

The proper way is the ordinary human process of noticing what has impressed you vividly and trying to associate it with the general appearance of the written page. Never mind if large tracts of the page or of the music are vague to you, both in the actual listening and in the reading; and do not expect that what makes a vivid impression on you will always be what is really important. My illustrations will come from the whole range of Beethoven's works, and as a rule I shall put in the forefront examples from the pianoforte works, because these will be accessible to most readers. Then I shall illustrate from the chamber music, and so on up to the largest orchestral and vocal works. Nothing is to be gained by classifying Beethoven's works according to their titles. It is quite absurd, for instance, to separate the sonatas from the trios, quartets, and symphonies. The term 'sonata' happens to have become limited to works for less than three instruments, but at least ninety per cent of Beethoven's work is in sonata form; and the whole of his aesthetic system has arisen from the sonata style, which is in itself a very large category of music, intimately associated with the revolution, or rather the birth, of dramatic musical style in the operas of Gluck.

Now let us take the plunge, and begin upon the study of Beethoven's tonality. Do not ask me for a definition of tonality. I have worked steadily at the subject itself, both as a practical composer and as a student of musical analysis, for over forty years, and while I have above defined it quite easily as a long-range view of harmony, I have not in my whole fifty years' study succeeded in making a description of it that would convey a clear idea to those who do not already understand it. But this need not worry us. When a difficulty amounts to an impossibility it is imaginary. I have elsewhere pointed out that the difficulty of defining tonality is the difficulty of describing any sensation whatever.

All I can do here to give the general reader clear ideas as to tonality is to tell him the facts of Beethoven's handling of it, and to give him opportunity of verifying my illustrations. Nine-tenths of the difficulty of this task consists in clearing away a mass of theoretical and speculative rubbish. To do this argumentatively would mean an enormous waste of space. In the presence of Beethoven I am not dogmatic. What Beethoven does I accept as evidence, but neither you nor I have time to deal with the theorists who would tell us that Beethoven ought to have done otherwise, or who try to prove that he acted according to their theories.

The first thing the general reader needs to know about tonality is that the names of keys do not represent important aesthetic facts. This statement is in evident conflict with various attractive and fantastic utterances by Beethoven himself and by other composers. Beethoven, for instance, when setting Scottish melodies, wrote to his Edinburgh publisher, Thomson, that the key of A flat did not fit a certain tune that was sent him, inasmuch as that tune was marked *amoroso*, whereas the key of A flat should be called *barbaresco*. Again, in one of his sketch-books, we have B minor referred to as 'black'. Curiously enough, all Beethoven's compositions in A flat are remarkably suave. About B minor we are hardly in a position to prove anything, as his only two important movements are that wonderful Scherzo, the fourth of his six *Bagatelles*, op. 126, which is certainly not black, and the *Agnus Dei* of the Mass in D, which one must admit to be a cry *de profundis*. But the fact is that all notions about the character of keys in themselves are of the order of things which psychologists study as 'number-forms' and colour associations. To me, the character of A flat is the character of most of the movements Beethoven wrote in that key. B minor I feel to be a not very dark brown, partly because of its relation to D minor, which I happen to think of as bright red, for reasons as inscrutable as those of the blind man who, on acquiring his sight through an operation, described scarlet as like the sound of a trumpet. But I also happen to feel that Friday is remarkably like the colour of A minor. This may perhaps be because I think of A minor as a fish-like white; but I have not the slightest idea why both Tuesday and E major should seem to me grass-green. E flat minor seems to me to be the colour of Bach's prelude in that key in Book I of the Forty-Eight; a very dark colour, because that is a very tragic piece. In Beethoven's case, the main reason why his fairly numerous movements in A flat have not the *barbaresco* character that he imputes to that key is that it comes in relation to C minor; and, as we shall soon see, it is not keys in themselves, but key-relations, that have character, and, moreover, a character that is deeply rooted and the same for all listeners. The slightest practical convenience will override Beethoven's most clearly stated notions of a key as having a character of its own. I have no more idea why F major seems pale pink to me than why E major seems grass-green. Nor have I either any recollection that Beethoven said anything about the character of these keys, or the slightest means of guessing what he would have said about them. But we do know that when he arranged his Pianoforte

Sonata, op. 14, no. 1, as a string quartet, he transposed it from E major to F major for reasons solely concerning the technique of the instruments. Gevaert, one of the most learned authorities on ancient music and the author of two monumental treatises on orchestration, considered that such a transposition would be equivalent to altering all the colours of a picture. He did not know this remarkable quartet-arrangement of Beethoven's, which was not published until some time after Gevaert's death, but his remarks on classical tonality are a favourable example of the kind of fantasy which many learned musicians still fail to confine to its proper place among psychological obscurities. In other words, he talks sad nonsense about tonality.

The character of keys in themselves is, then, a psychological vagary about which no two persons need trouble to agree. Key-relationship, on the other hand, is the source of an enormous proportion of Beethoven's harmonic colour effects, and is one of the primary elements in his form. You see that I am already driven to use metaphors, and I shall continue to speak of key-relations as 'dark' or 'bright' and 'high' or 'dull' in colour. These metaphors will not be fancies, but verifiable musical experience. They are quite unaffected by transposition; and you need not have a sense of 'absolute pitch' to enjoy them. In the little E major Sonata, op. 14, No. 1, the C major key of the trio of the middle Allegretto brings with it a pleasant darkness and warmth in relation to E minor, which is exactly the same as the D flat which it becomes in relation to the F minor of that movement as arranged for string quartet, and, incidentally, exactly the same as the 'barbarous' key of A flat in relation to the C minor with which Beethoven almost always brings it into contact.

I write in the hope that this book will be read, as I know that many of my analytical essays have been read, by persons who cannot read musical notation. But for such persons the present discussion will be unintelligible without the help of friends who can illustrate it on the pianoforte. The phenomena of short-range tonality can be easily and quickly illustrated. Those of long range cannot be seen except in whole compositions; but the difficulty of learning to appreciate them is nothing like what it was before the days of broadcasting and the gramophone.

Let us begin with the short-range, or local, phenomena. The reader need not cumber his conscience with philosophic doubts about the definition of 'scale'. If he runs his finger along the white keys of the pianoforte, he will obtain a diatonic scale which is not in mathematically perfect tune, but is tempered so as to comprise a tolerable average of our harmonic needs in twelve notes to the octave. Run your fingers along the black keys, and you will obtain a pentatonic scale, such as is characteristic of many Scotch melodies and of much other folk music widely distributed among the races of mankind.

Your diatonic scale on the white notes will satisfy your instinct for key only when each octave of it runs from C to C. This produces the scale of C major. All other cross-sections will seem to you out of balance, though you may have enough experience of the music of the sixteenth century to recognize in them the qualities of the Church modes, and you will hardly have escaped encountering them in the stylistic efforts and affectations of modern music.

Your pentatonic scale on the black notes will prove to be a selection from the diatonic scale if its octaves run from F sharp to F sharp.

For the minor mode, the reader who cannot read musical notation must rely upon illustrations. Minor scales are unstable affairs that cannot be described without going into tiresome grammatical details. The tonic-sol-fa system may have simplified its practice, but has hopelessly falsified its theory and contradicted its name, by treating A minor as the minor form ('Lah mode') of C major. The first thing that must be recognized about classical tonality is that the *tonic*, whether major or minor, is, so to speak, the listener's home. A composition in a minor key, say C minor, will always present some elements of emotional conflict so long as it remains in the minor mode, but it will have ended at home whether it ends in C minor or C major. If it 'modulates' into E flat, it has changed its key. The listener cannot exaggerate the importance of this feeling of change of key. The return to what I shall call the home tonic is a matter, not of mere symmetry and balance, but of first-rate dramatic importance in all the music comprised between the periods of Haydn and Wagner. Wagner was thought by his contemporary critics, and by some people nowadays, to have got beyond classical tonality, but his very transcendence of it depends on his firm grasp of its principles.

The most naïve listener can easily be convinced that he has a harmonic sense of the tonic and its essential finality. All he needs is to have *God Save the King* played to him with the wrong final chord, not necessarily a discord or a nonsensical chord, but one such as would constitute an 'interrupted' cadence.

When we come to tonality *in extenso*, the uninformed listener may expect to find more difficulty in recognizing the facts, but I can reassure him that the sane classical composer makes no such demands upon the human memory as might be inferred from the statements of text-books. There are cases in classical music where a return to the home tonic, or to any other key of importance, is likely to escape recognition: there is not a single case in which the composer has neglected to associate a return with overwhelming collateral evidence when he wishes it to be recognized. And, in the cases where it is not recognizable except by a more or less professional sense of absolute pitch, there is always a subtlety in the fact that the listener is harmonically at home without having noticed it; unless, of course, the work is not a masterpiece. It is bad policy to try and recognize subtleties before you can recognize the great simplicities. There is no limit to the subtleties of Beethoven's tonality, and I shall point them out as they occur. It is my belief that a listener without knowledge of musical notation needs only time and experience to appreciate them all; but, of course, the trained musician can give him a very long start in the race towards this goal. On the other hand, the trained musician carries a heavy weight of theoretic lore, most of which is unaesthetic, even where it happens to be correct.

In order to give the facts of tonality names at all, I must here set down the ABC, or rather the CDEFGAB, in words and notes. Some readers of detective stories have the patience to study the map which in the more clockwork mysteries shows the topography of the scene of the crime. The reader who has no use for my tables, printed on the following pages will be better advised not to study it at all directly, but at once to make himself acquainted with the passages from Beethoven and other composers which I shall now discuss to illustrate its details.

First, let us be quite clear about the contrast between tonic minor and tonic major. Remember that the contrast is not a 'modulation' or change of key at all: it is a change of outlook while we stay at home. The two modes must be heard in juxtaposition, as between two sonata movements, or between minuet and trio, or between main theme and episode in a rondo. Without separately counting immediate returns after the change, you can find some twenty-six cases of contrast between tonic major and minor as between whole sections in Beethoven's sonatas. On the smallest scale of all, you will find the archaic *tierce de Picardie* at the end of many movements of Bach in the minor mode. To unsophisticated listeners it comes almost as a shock. Nothing in Bach is merely archaic, and we must always be on our guard against confusing historic origins with aesthetic values; but, historically, the *tierce de Picardie* originates in the fact that the tonality of the various minor modes of sixteenth-century music is so unstable that a minor triad has far less finality than a bare fifth or octave. If a third was to be admitted at all, it had to be a major third. You will not find the *tierce de Picardie* in Haydn, Mozart, or Beethoven, because, with these composers, if a piece in a minor key is going to end in a major at all, it will establish itself firmly therein some time before the end.

You will find in the Sonatas, opp. 90 and 111, that Beethoven satisfies you and himself perfectly by having his first movement in a minor key and his finale in the tonic major. The triumphant C major Finale of the Fifth Symphony and the choral Finale of the Ninth Symphony are his other leading cases in this matter. It is possible for a composition in a major key to end in the tonic minor, but there is no such case in Beethoven. Mendelssohn's

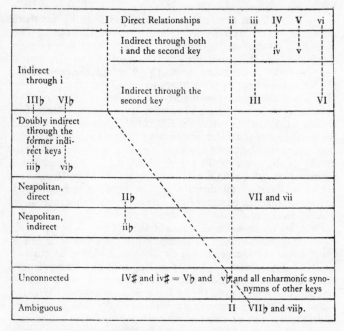

	I	Direct Relationships	ii	iii	IV	V	vi
		Indirect through both i and the second key			iv	v	
Indirect through i III♭ VI♭		Indirect through the second key		III			VI
Doubly indirect through the former indirect keys iii♭ vi♭							
Neapolitan, direct		II♭		VII and vii			
Neapolitan, indirect		ii♭					
Unconnected		IV♯ and iv♯ = V♭ and	v♭ and all enharmonic synonymns of other keys				
Ambiguous				II	VII♭ and vii♭.		

Italian Symphony and Brahms's B major Trio, op. 8, in both its versions, are our main leading cases for this. There are one or two smaller pieces, such as Schubert's Impromptu in E flat, op. 90, No. 2, and Brahms's Rhapsody, op. 119, No. 4, and there is a Nocturne in B major by Chopin, op. 32, No. 1, which ends with a very dramatic recitative of which the last chord is minor, a fact which has so shocked many editors that they have bowdlerized it into major.

We now come to the most important key-centre next to the tonic—viz. the dominant (V), without which no tonic can get itself established. The dominant chord is penultimate in every full close. Its third provides the leading note of the scale and must be major even where the mode is minor. Extraordinary subtleties of tonality hinge upon the functions of the dominant.

The composer who worked them out with supreme subtlety was Mozart. Beethoven so enormously extended and rationalized the whole system of key-relations that the extreme subtleties of the dominant became crowded out and tend in his later works rather to be replaced by methods of avoiding the dominant altogether. The listener cannot too soon become familiar with the use of the

	ı	Direct Relationships	IIIb	iv	v	VIb	VIIb
		Indirect through both I and the second key		IV	V		
Indirect through ı iii♯ vi♯		Indirect through the second key	iib			vib	
Doubly indirect through the former indirect keys III♯—VI♯							
Neapolitan, direct		IIb					
Neapolitan, indirect		iib				VII♯ and vii♯	
Unconnected		IV♯ and iv♯ =	Vb and vb and all enharmonic synonyms of other keys				
Ambiguous	ii	II vib					

dominant as a means of rousing expectations of the tonic. There is no hurry for him to qualify as a trustworthy independent observer of the facts. A vast mass of analytical commentary has been written by apparently learned writers who are quite incompetent in this matter, but I am convinced that a familiarity with suitable illustrations will soon give every reader an admirably vivid idea of the essential point.

I have already said that the dominant is the ordinary penultimate chord for every full close. Most chords that keep within the range of the diatonic scale can be harmonized with little difficulty on the chords of the tonic and dominant. You can harmonize *God Save the King* on that repertoire without absolute incorrectness, though I do not recommend the procedure, and pages and pages of Rossini's *Barbiere* live upon nothing else. Now, if the dominant is the ordinary penultimate chord for full closes, it follows that prolonged harping on the dominant will arouse expectation of the tonic; and, moreover, that, if you approach any major triad from some remote quarter or from nowhere, and harp upon it for a considerable time, it is more likely to sound like a dominant than a tonic, and if you add a seventh to it you will confirm that impression beyond doubt.

The first lesson in Beethoven's tonality is, then, the following riddle:

    Q. When is a key not a key?
    A. When it's a dominant.

The easiest illustration of this may be found in a sonata which is one of the first given to young pianists—the first movement of Beethoven's op. 14, no. 2.

Take bars 19–25 and play them without their context.

Ex.1

They themselves give no evidence that they are not in A major, and plenty of commentaries on Beethoven have been published in which such a passage will be described as in A major. Let us have all such commentaries burnt by the common hangman. Take the passage in its context, play the movement from the beginning, and stop at the four A's in bar 25. There is a legend that, when the infant Mozart insisted on lying slug-abed, he could always be got out of bed if you played a scale which stopped on the leading note. You may not feel as strongly as Mozart on this matter, but you will certainly feel a kindred irritation if bar 25 of Beethoven's Sonata, op. 14, no. 2, is not followed by a chord of D. The previous passage was not in A major at all. It was what I shall call an enhanced dominant. The composer wishes to establish the actual key of the dominant, D major, so firmly that his home tonic, G major, sinks below the horizon. The key of D major is merely the dominant of G, and there is no drawing a firm line between using it as a chord in G major and actually going into it and surrounding it with its own accessories. To establish it as a new key from which you do not intend to return, you must not only harp upon its dominant, but give that dominant its own dominant details, such as the G sharps. 'Dominant preparation' is the term for showing the intention of settling in a key, whether that be a new key or the home tonic.[1]

Passages that prepare for the advent of a new key are essentially like well-worked-out preparations for the first entry of an important character in a drama. Much more exciting, though not different in harmonic structure, are the passages that prepare for the return to the home tonic. Let us begin for convenience with one of the most exciting—that in the first movement of the 'Waldstein' Sonata, op. 53, bars 136–155. You will not appreciate the full force of this until you hear it in its place in the whole movement, and the 'Waldstein' Sonata is enormously more difficult to play than most people think. (Beethoven suffers cruelly from teachers and players who have not outgrown the delusion that the difficulty of a piece is to be gauged by the presence or absence of types of passage which come sooner or later in one's technical studies.)

In later works, Beethoven discovered that there are more exciting ways of returning to the home tonic. We shall do well to mistrust the common explanation that he grew tired of the dominant or was anxious to get away from it, or even the explanation, more flattering to ourselves, that the listener grows more intelligent and less in need of such explanatory devices. We shall never understand a work of art unless we take it as a whole. And it is only small and incomplete artists whose way of broadening from precedent to precedent is to narrow from boredom to boredom. Dominant preparation becomes crowded out of Beethoven's works because his wider harmonic range has made it inadequate. The history of the 'Waldstein' Sonata itself exquisitely demonstrates the process, for the new harmonic wealth of its first movement and Finale crowded out the very beautiful Andante in F which Beethoven afterwards published separately, substituting for it the single page called *Introduzione* which now stands in the Sonata and is harmonically its richest feature.

But, within two years of composing the 'Waldstein' Sonata, Beethoven already transcended it in precisely its most exciting passage by the similar passage in the first movement of one of his smaller symphonies, the Fourth Symphony in B flat, op. 60, in each case the return to the recapitulation.

People who can play pianoforte duets should not despise the

---

[1] In the original typescript there is an indication that the author intended to quote here 'a list of the most undisguised passages of dominant preparation in the sonatas of Beethoven'. No such list was compiled, however.

humble four-hand arrangements of symphonies. The non-musician needs every variety of stimulus to his imagination that he can get, and the stimulus of taking an active part in music is of all stimulants the least liable to become a narcotic.

As in the 'Waldstein' Sonata, and such cases, the passage is merely a more or less exciting noise, unless you hear it in its place in the movement as a whole, and here you may as well take in the slow introduction as well. You will find the passage very much more exciting than that in the 'Waldstein' Sonata. In the first place, the chord on which the drum-roll begins has come from nowhere, and not only from nowhere, but through a process of mystification known to grammarians as an 'enharmonic modulation'; but the essential point in which this passage is far more powerful than anything in the 'Waldstein' Sonata is that it is not on a dominant chord and does not sound as if it were. It is the chord of the home tonic itself, and the excitement of the whole crescendo comes from the growing realization that we have been at home all the time long before we realized it. That is one reason why you will appreciate this passage in the Fourth Symphony better if you have played the Introduction as well as the Allegro. For the crash that breaks in upon the mysterious Introduction and leads to the Allegro is a crash on the ordinary dominant, and so you have within the work itself a means of comparing that more normal procedure with the surprise of finding yourself actually in the home tonic without an explanatory dominant.

Before going farther, it is as well to realize how inseparable are these matters of key-preparation from matters of musical form. What force would either of these passages have had if, instead of returning to what you cannot fail to recognize as the main theme, they had been followed by some new idea? In these passages, such an event would be as nonsensical as the conclusion of the detective story in which the murder turns out to have been committed by a hitherto unmentioned nonentity who crept into the concealed chamber by an unsuspected tunnel from the village inn. The music-lover need have no fear that the classical composer expects from him, or from the most experienced musician, a sense of tonality that is capable of recognizing a return to the home tonic without an overwhelmingly cogent appeal to his memory and to other grounds of expectation.

Now let us turn to one of the most famous arousings of expectation in all music—the miraculous passage from the Finale of the Fifth Symphony. Here we have a preparation, not for a return, but for the dawn of something quite new. The third movement (technically describable as the scherzo, though it is anything but a joke) is finished, exhausted, played out. It has consisted of a main section, dark, mysterious, and, in part, fierce, which we may call the scherzo proper. This has suddenly collapsed in a quiet full close, just before the double bar and the change to C major that you will find in the middle of the movement. Its trio is a rumbustious affair in grotesque high spirits. The trio dies away, and the return to the scherzo is one of the ghostliest things ever written, with something of the thin, bickering quality of the poor ghosts that Homer describes where Odysseus visits the Land of Shadows.

This *da capo* is shortened by leaving out its middle modulations. It reaches the penultimate chords before the trio. But the cadence is interrupted—that is to say, the final tonic chord is undermined. And now comes the famous passage with the innumerable quiet drum-taps which, as Parry long ago pointed out, is a miracle in its place and quite meaningless in isolation. The drum, as you will see, is upon the tonic note, but the bass hovers uneasily to and fro beneath it; and, finally, we have the paradox of the tonic in the drums, quasi-dominant harmonies above it, and the dominant below it, until only at the imminent approach of the crash the top-heavy harmony straightens itself out into a dominant seventh. If you stop before the finale begins, you will assuredly find that you do not expect a return to anything that you have heard before. There is no question that the scherzo is played out. What you would expect, without being wise after the event, I do not know. It is quite certain that the enormous blaze of the triumphant finale is what you need.

But this is not the final consummation of Beethoven's stroke of genius. Triumphs, once begun, are mainly processional affairs, and in processions dramatic events tend to be subversive and deplorable. Yet Beethoven has at the height of his triumph an event which is neither. The nearest approach to its effect in history is, I venture to think, Kipling's action in publishing his *Recessional* the day after the Diamond Jubilee, though I am far from implying that Beethoven's intention in any piece of music can be more than dimly illustrated by anything either in history or literature; but the motto 'Lest we forget' is an admirable summary of the effect which Beethoven produces when, at the end of his development, he is preparing quite formally on the dominant for a return to his main theme. There is not, and cannot be, anything exciting about this. There is nothing to be done with the dominant preparation but to see that the rhythms march well, that the top notes have a satisfactory ring, and that the big chords are nobly spaced. But then comes the silence, measured, rather than broken, by the dying swing of the rhythm. The most pregnant of the scherzo themes is heard again. By means of delicate differences in scoring and continuation, it has acquired a character for which it had no leisure in its original terrifying surroundings. It is a memory of the past, not a re-capture of it. Without undue sentimentality, we can pity ourselves for past terrors, and even a hero's reference to them may take a pathetic tone. Soon there is a crescendo leading to the recapitulation section, which means the procession with a triumphal march again at the beginning. But this preparation, though subtly pathetic in tone, is harmonically the most ordinary affair of twenty-four pulses on the dominant.

In all these matters (and they are the most difficult problems in art), Beethoven is supremely right, as surely as sensational and sentimental artists are wrong. I must inflict one more technical detail upon the non-professional reader, in order to save future trouble in describing similar passages. It is quite clear that the beginning of that passage from the 'Waldstein' Sonata is on and around a chord on the triad of G, which might, apart from its context, mean the key of G major as long as we do not add a seventh to it. As soon as F natural appears (four bars before the return), it becomes a dominant seventh, and can be nothing but what the context has already proved it to be, the dominant of C. Now, in the passage in the Fourth Symphony, you will find yourself entirely without any feeling that the chord of B flat is anything but a tonic chord. The reason for this is that in its first appearance it is what is known as a 6/4, or second inversion, of the triad—that is to say, in the present case its bass is F. The G flat of the previous chord has fallen to F, the D flat and E natural have risen respectively to D natural and F, B flat has been common to both chords. This is the normal behaviour of the chord known as the augmented sixth, but it would have been grammatically possible to avoid putting F at the bottom of the first B flat major chord, and then the passage would have been markedly unstable. It might have been as dominant, for all we can tell, as the first thunder-rolls in the passage in the 'Waldstein' Sonata. But the F at the bottom has given us all the dominant we want. If you have the misfortune to dabble in musical theory, classical or modern, you will encounter much obscurity and nervous legislation about this 6/4 chord. You may neglect all that, if you will realize that the whole trouble arises from its having been defined as the second inversion of a triad. A chord is inverted when its root, a question-begging term which I decline to discuss here, is not in the bass, and a chord of three notes will obviously have two inversions.

Ex.2

Unfortunately, in ninety-nine cases out of a hundred, your 6/4 chord coincides with the second inversion of a triad by mere accident. In the ninety-nine cases it is a double *appoggiatura*—that is to say, an ornamental discord leaning upon the essential note on which it is to resolve. The first stage in the evolution of this unfortunate 6/4 is the following manifest discord and the 5/4 suspension.

Ex. 3

And the second stage is when you give the fifth a leading note of its own.

The fact that there is no actual discord in the sound of the 6/4 chord does not make the expression less metaphorical than an actual harshness, the fact being that discord in highly organized music is not so much a question of sound as of sense, a discord being in Wagner's most complex cases like a very compressed metaphor, and in the simplest cases like a transitive verb which needs an object if the sentence which contains it is to be complete. So you see that in the Fourth Symphony Beethoven strikes his home tonic in a manner which is already dominant. He allows that impression to die away so soon, and spaces out his crescendo so widely, that there is a very effective surprise in finding oneself at home without having rung the door-bell. In the passage in the C minor Symphony, he has put his dominant below his tonic and arranged for an acute conflict, not only between his tonic drum and his dominant harmonies, but also with the dawn of a strong implication of the subdominant as well.

We must now discuss the subdominant. Here, again, I venture to hope that the non-technical reader will derive vivid impressions of the facts as soon as he can contrive by any means to hear the musical illustrations I shall give. The illustrations given in harmony text-books are of no conceivable use, because they merely consist of horrid little progressions on the scale of *A Cat Sat on a Mat*, and when they give classical examples they cannot afford, any more than we can here, to print them in their contexts. We cannot too often remind ourselves that Beethoven's enormous extension of the range of harmony is a function of his enormous extension of the whole range of musical form and expression; and that even an 'interesting' progression, or 'licence', in a couple of chords is a thing for which explanation will hardly be forthcoming in less than a whole movement.

Our ideas about the subdominant will become much clearer if we think of it as the anti-dominant. In the scale it happens, unfortunately, to be the note below the dominant, and we

therefore accept its name in the belief that it corresponds to that
of the supertonic, as the note which really is nothing but the note
above the tonic. But the subdominant should be thought of as
a fifth below the tonic, and this will explain to us the term
'submediant', for the mediant is the note which lies midway
between the tonic and the dominant, and so the submediant is
that which lies midway between the tonic and the subdominant.
Now you will always find that going to the key of the dominant
is an active measure. It is going forward, and the key of the
dominant sounds brighter than that of the tonic, however much
you may neutralize it by the tone of your dominant passages in
other respects. Similarly, returning from the dominant to the
tonic has always something of the aspect of a descent, even
though the surface of the music may rise. You look down upon
your tonic from the slightly higher level of your dominant. (I am
not, of course, speaking of musical pitch at all.) Now, to the
key of the subdominant, your home tonic is dominant. The
obvious results of this are important. Your subdominant is a
region of repose and retirement. A composition of which the
first important and established change of key is the subdominant
will hardly be more than a lyric movement, with that change of
key as its only episode. In larger and more active movements,
the normal place for asserting the subdominant with any emphasis
is near the end. And the most characteristic of all uses of the
subdominant is that known as the 'plagal cadence', which imparts

Ex. 4

the solemnity of an *Amen* to the end after the normal full close
has finished the story. Hence my strong suspicion, which I have
expressed in other writings, that the chord of the subdominant
was really the Lost Chord which the uneasy organist could not
find again, and that the organist probably did, in fact, stumble
upon it many times both before and since, but without happening
to bring it into subdominant relation to its tonic; for you cannot
dwell long upon any major chord without beginning to suspect
that it may be a dominant instead of a tonic.

Beethoven's First Symphony shocked the pedants by beginning
quite definitely in the key of its subdominant with its first two
chords. In a few more chords it established its proper tonic of
C major by firmly modulating to its dominant and there remaining
for some time, not as in the key of that dominant, but as on the

dominant as a bass. The pedants need not have been shocked.
John Sebastian Bach was still undiscovered by most of them, but
his son, Carl Philipp Emanuel Bach, was accepted as a classic, and
had on a small scale gone much farther with such experiments
than Beethoven ever did. Many pieces of music impart a certain
wistfulness to their openings by a strong subdominant bias. It is
one of the commonest features of the great Bach's style, which
you may find in three obvious cases in his Forty-Eight Preludes
and Fugues: Book I, Preludes 7 and 11, and Book II, Prelude 1;
and much more often in his larger works. Bach does not go as
far as Beethoven's First Symphony in striking the flat seventh
at the very beginning of the bar, but he proceeds exactly like
Beethoven in giving you enough dominant afterwards to establish
his tonic beyond doubt. Thus, it is evident that a piece of music
needs room to recover from an emphatic subdominant. In
Anglican chanting, it would be hardly possible for a single chant
to modulate to the subdominant without thereby seeming itself
to be a mere hovering on the dominant of that key, and even a
double chant would hardly have time to recover. The effect
might pass for an essay in the Mixolydian mode, but most members
of the congregation would feel puzzled, if edified.

In the Allegretto of Beethoven's Eighth Symphony, the subdominant appears in a most normal course of events, beginning
with a recapitulation of a passage of six bars that has previously
returned from the dominant to the home tonic (bars 35–40). To
recapitulate these bars *on* the home tonic (not *in* it) is, of course,
to assert the subdominant, and Beethoven continues to play
humorously with this subdominant for six bars more. He then
has three bars of self-repeating final cadence, with a crescendo in
burlesque imitation of the already notoriously burlesque style of
Rossinian opera. Some musicians feel quite strongly that this
has not re-established his tonic, and that nothing short of what I
have already called an enhanced dominant could restore the
balance. I have not myself noticed that the end of this movement
is thus left floating in the air, but those who feel it to be so are
entitled to enjoy the sensation as a characteristic example of
Beethoven's humour. I have already remarked that even our best
modern writers on Beethoven seem not to appreciate the fact that
humour is one of Beethoven's most highly developed characteristics. But it would be rash to accuse any writer of failing to
describe Beethoven's humour, for what can be more fatal to a joke
than to analyse it, especially if the analysis must be musical? I
cannot help that. Beethoven without his humour is as inconceivable as a humourless Shakespeare. His tragic power would
lose half its cogency if he were not the most drastic of realists and
disillusionizers as to the relation between tragedy and comedy.

The very fact that the subdominant is a point of repose makes it one of the most characteristic supports of a melodic climax. The obviously right chord for the top note in the penultimate bar of *God Save the King* is the chord of the subdominant, followed of course, by the usual 6/4—5/3 full close into the tonic.

Take the sublime melody of the Andante in Beethoven's Trio in B flat, op. 97, and you will find that its top note at the beginning of the last four bars is that of a subdominant chord. Again, take the more elaborate and not less sublime principal melody of the Adagio of the Ninth Symphony. You will find that its climax is on the subdominant (bars 15, 16, reproduced in bars 21, 22). I shall have reason for recurring to these two great melodies later on.

Ex.5

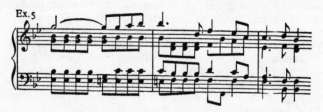

Towards the end of the Adagio of the Ninth Symphony, the sub-dominant appears with dramatic, instead of merely melodic, emphasis, but the force of this I cannot properly explain until we have almost finished our survey of Beethoven's tonality.

The other key centres are less important and less definite in their effect, but there are plenty of professional musicians, as well as non-musicians, who would be none the worse for a little practice in identifying them. First of all, let us get rid of the implications of the current terms 'relative minor' and 'relative major'. The key of A minor is called the relative minor of C, and C major is called the relative major of A minor. Relative minors and majors happen to use the same key signature, a mere matter of typo-graphical convenience. They are no more closely related than the rest of the five related keys.

Now let us begin to illustrate our tiresome map of the scene of the crime, an enjoyable enough process if the reader can contrive to hear the examples cited. Take the scale of C major and put a common chord on each of its degrees,

Ex.6

without going outside the scale and excluding the discordant im-perfect triad on B. Direct key-relationship consists simply in the fact that the tonic chord of one key is among the common chords of the other. With Bach and Handel, unless the music is working miracles, as in Bach's Chromatic Fantasia and 'Thy rebuke hath broken his heart' in *Messiah*, changes of key are not essentially more dramatic than incidents in an ordinary melody, and the need of a return to the home tonic is only the need for decorative symmetry. In my analysis [1] of one of Beethoven's most original works, the overture *Die Weihe des Hauses*, op. 124, I have described how Beethoven is compelled by the aesthetics of orchestral fugue-writing to return to Bach's and Handel's treatment of keys, like the tournament horses in *Alice Through the Looking-Glass*, who let the White Knight and Red Knight get on and off them as if they were tables.

Now, from any major tonic, you can modulate to any of the five keys represented by its other triads without the slightest shock to the flow of your melody. To surround each triad with its own local dominant is merely to emphasize it, and nothing is more destructive to the student's sense of form than the custom, not yet obsolete, of calling every one of these incidents a change of key, unless it be the still worse custom of setting as an examination question the task of writing some twenty bars making such-and-such modulations, when neither the student nor the examiner has the slightest idea why a real composer should do any such thing.

For reasons which will appear later, the supertonic is not often established as a related key on a large scale, but modulations to it in the course of melody are quite common. In the G major Sonata, op. 14, no. 2, the second and third bars would be in the supertonic but for the fact that the bass has remained fixed on the tonic. If the bass had moved up to A via G sharp, the opening would have become more fussy, but would have retained the same sense. It is opportune to remark here that an enormous range of harmony can be allowed freedom to expand in this way above such a fixed bass, which will be either a tonic or a dominant pedal.

In the Adagio of op. 2, no. 3, you will find the supertonic employed on quite a large scale by way of repeating bars 1 and 2 in sequence a step higher in bars 5 and 6. And you will find the same device equally clearly in the reciprocity between the first eight and the second eight bars of the Minuet in opus 10, no. 3. (A musical sequence is the repetition of some member of a phrase in orderly succession at different pitches.)

The best illustrations of openings that display the supertonic do not happen to come in Beethoven's Pianoforte Sonatas, but in the Allegro of the First Symphony, where the procedure is a very formal, businesslike affair, and the supertonic eventually reaches

[1] *Essays in Musical Analysis*, vol. II.

the dominant via the subdominant (see Ex. 9, p. 31); and much
more tersely within a single broad phrase of a majestically quiet
melody at the opening of the C major String Quintet, op. 29.

Ex.7

There is no reason why the mediant (iii) should not often be
emphasized as a local key-relation or a detail of melody, but there
is less occasion for it than there is for the supertonic. Modulating
to the supertonic means taking your musical figure sequentially
up one step of your scale, a commoner procedure than a sequence
that rises by thirds, if only because it involves a much greater
contrast of harmony. (By the way, you must not be misled either
by melodies or basses in this matter. You have not moved to the
supertonic merely if the bass has moved up to that note, even if
the melody has moved with it: e.g. the second bar of the Sonata,
op. 110, has nothing to do with the supertonic. Its harmony is
one of the inversions of the dominant seventh.)

There is a beautiful mediant modulation in the Allegretto of the
String Quartet in D major, op. 18, no. 3. I cannot find anything
like it in the Pianoforte Sonatas, but, if you take another example
already quoted, the Allegretto of the Sonata, op. 14, no. 1, and
pretend that its C major trio is the beginning of the piece, you will
find the effect of the move from C back to the initial E minor a
very good illustration. And the Finale of the E minor String
Quartet, op. 59, no. 2, placed in circumstances where every
listener will expect it to be in E minor, insists on making the very
same point by obstinately beginning in C major and returning to
that key again and again from its proper E minor with a jerk as
vicious as that of any carter pulling his cart out of a rut. Here
again is a glorious instance of Beethoven's humour in a work which
on the whole is a good deal nearer to tragedy than to comedy.

The subdominant (IV) we have already dealt with. You will
find the so-called relative minor, the submediant (vi), no more
prominent than the other relative keys. On a large scale, as in
choice of key for a slow movement, for a rondo episode, for the
trio of a minuet, etc., statistics will no doubt show more examples
than for other keys, and the juxtaposition of the minuets and
scherzos of op. 2, no. 3, op. 28, and op. 22, with their trios,
will give you all you want to know of their effect, whether on a
large scale or a small.

It now remains to give the key-relations of a minor tonic. The working out of these is full of tiresome grammatical details with which I will not trouble the reader. But the net result of it is that you can turn my set of six triads backwards and reckon from the A minor triad. This does not prove the tonic-sol-fa-ists' contention that A minor is the Lah-mode of C. There is simply no sense in classical music if the key of C major has any other minor mode but C minor. In my table I have given the names and the Roman figures of the key-relations from A minor. If we are to work out Beethoven's enormous extension of the old classical range of key-relations, the reader will find it convenient for reference to translate these minor relations into C minor.

The first paradox that we encounter is this: that, while the dominant chord of a minor key must be major in order to make full closes with their leading notes possible at all, the dominant key is certainly minor. There are theorists who will reason against this convention, under the mistaken belief that human beings and works of art can trust in logic before they know all the premisses. We can save ourselves the trouble of arguing about this by seeing what will happen to the opening of a Bach fugue in a minor key if we answer its subject in the dominant major. Here are the first three entries in the sixteenth fugue of the first book of Bach's Forty-eight. You see that he answers his subject in the dominant minor, and that he needs an extra bar in which to get smoothly back to the home tonic for his third entry. (At all events, he likes extra bars and does not believe that a fugue should scan like a limerick.)

Ex. 8

Now consider how you would like an answer in the dominant major. You may take it that, for purposes of modulation—that is, for change of key—the dominant key of a minor key is always minor. That being so, the subdominant key will also be minor. It is the key to which the home tonic is dominant; but now notice a peculiarity of the minor subdominant with powerful emotional effects. The popular notion that the minor mode is always melancholy is no doubt crude. Gluck, one of the greatest pioneers in consciously and dramatically emotional music, relies upon the major mode for his highest pathos and uses the minor mode always to express conflict, and conflict the minor mode always will express. Its harmonic necessities are full of conflicts. A change from the minor mode to a related major key will normally bring the contrast of something calmer, and will therefore seem to administer consolation to whatever pathetic elements may have been present. This is conspicuous enough in the Allegretto of op. 14, no. 1; but the tonic major, as can be seen in the Sonata, op. 2, no. 1, in the E minor Sonata, op. 90, and in the glorious triumph of the Fifth Symphony, is not mere consolation. It is a definite removal of all cause of conflict in their very place of origin. Now when you are in a minor key, you cannot go straight into its subdominant without using the dominant chord thereof, and that dominant chord must be major. In other words, modulation from a minor tonic to its subdominant key means the tragic irony of a momentary major tonic chord, implying a hope which is frustrated at the very moment by the flattened seventh, which leads us to a still darker minor key. Even a final major third will not remove the pathetic impression of its harmonic irony. You will find it at its highest pathos in the eighth prelude of Book I of Bach's Forty-Eight, and on a very large scale in the last fourteen bars of the Adagio of Beethoven's Sonata, op. 106. Other examples in Bach, Beethoven, and Brahms are so numerous and so characteristic that most readers will soon find little difficulty in noticing them as they arise.

There is no related key on the supertonic of the minor mode. Instead we have the converse relation, the flat seventh. To the use of this on a large scale there are hindrances similar to those of the large-scale use of the supertonic of a major key. These will be expanded in the next chapter, but Beethoven has opportunely provided us with two very conspicuous examples: first, in the slow movement of his D major Trio, op. 70, no. 1, a movement in D minor with a second group in C major; and, secondly, in the Scherzo of the Ninth Symphony, in the main body of which quite a large second group in C major is contrasted with the main theme in D minor. There is nothing to prevent the use of the key of the flat seventh in the course of melodies except the fact that it will be difficult to distinguish that key from a mere dominant of the mediant (III), the so-called relative major. If you can avoid returning from the flat seventh to the tonic via the mediant, you will get the peculiarly bleak desolation achieved by Schubert near the beginning of his wonderful 'Gretchen am Spinnrade'. Modulations to this mediant are so normal as to need no mention. It is the first key to which a movement of development in a minor key will normally proceed if it intends to go to a major key at all.

The other remaining key is, of course, the submediant, somewhat darker in colour than the mediant, probably because, in any extended passage, the mediant will be its dominant, and the ear will have some appreciation of the relation of both to the home tonic. Do not, however, place much reliance on the capacity of the ear to recognize merely harmonic relations across a wide area of intervening events. There is no limit to a great composer's power to produce long-distance actions. Wagner's are perfectly cogent across his four days' tetralogy of *The Ring*. But these long-distance effects were not produced by harmonic abstractions, and the composers and critics who believe that they can recognize such abstractions by ear are attaching an enormously exaggerated aesthetic importance to a sense of absolute pitch which they may or may not possess. There is more harm than at first sight appears in seeing imaginary values in music, for it is hardly possible to attend to such imaginings without losing one's capacity to see the facts. I retain an obstinate hope that the most general of readers will with time and patience develop his own sense of the facts that I am trying to describe, but he will do so all the quicker if he skips any and every passage in my argument which he cannot verify by the illustrations. On the other hand, no one need wait in the expectation that the effects I describe are going to be startling. It is not the purpose of this book to teach musical grammar. If I were discussing Greek or German literature, I would not willingly mention the nominative and the accusative, but readers of books on music are in urgent need of protection from commentaries which proceed like a person who should discourse about emotional values in Greek drama while making frequent mistakes about who killed whom.

THE LARGER TONALITY

THE identity of tonic major and tonic minor is one of the most important facts in tonality, perhaps the most important. As we have already seen, the sixteenth-century composer, whose harmonic perspective was less solid than the perspective of the Primitive painters before Giotto, could not achieve any finality in a minor triad, and so, if he was writing in a minor mode, had either to make his last chord with no third at all, or a major *tierce de Picardie*. As tonality became more solid, the various minor modes settled down to the one form now familiar. Even that form is very much less stable than the major mode, and we have already seen that key-relationships from a minor tonic are rather the keys to which that tonic is related than vice versa. The sixteenth-century *tierce de Picardie* begins to sound unexpected in Bach, though he uses it more often than not. But it has become unexpected only because the change from the unstable and somewhat acid harmonies of the minor mode to the brightness and stability of the major mode has become a distinctly emotional effect for which we expect some preparation and some confirmation afterwards. Beyond every minor key lurks the possibility of its tonic major bursting through, and, if the home tonic is minor, its transformation to major is an event at home and not abroad. Now, Beethoven extended the range of tonality by adding the relations of his tonic major to those of his tonic minor and vice versa. This leaves so few distances out in the cold that the superficial doctrine has arisen which, under the slogan of 'the unity of the chromatic scale', teaches that nothing but convention keeps the remotest keys outside. Such a doctrine entirely misses the drastic simplicity and clearness with which Beethoven and all great composers tell us when and how two keys are related. If the listener takes any interest in the subject at all, an enormous burden will fall off his conscience when he realizes that in classical music no two keys are related through the medium of a third tonic, and that no sense of key-relation arises except between keys that are in immediate juxtaposition. Most musicians probably have enough sense of absolute pitch to recognize that two widely separated passages are in the same key, but when they imagine that this recognition is a genuine aesthetic experience they are like persons who, having been told what masterpieces of painting are admirable in proportion and composition, practise measuring the details of such pictures with a foot-rule until they have acquired a skill in estimating the distances to a millimetre by eye. One of the greatest musicians I have ever known, whose own compositions display the highest mastery of tonality, had never noticed until I mentioned it to him that the brilliant new theme that appears after the first episode in Chopin's third *Ballade* is in the home tonic. We do not expect a return to the home tonic to be associated with a theme we have never heard before, any more than we expect on returning from our holiday to find our house completely redecorated and refurnished and inhabited by total strangers. Of course, if a piece asserts its keys in the dramatic manner of sonatas and then frequently returns from remote regions to the home tonic without explanation, there will arise either a subtlety or a merely weak harmonic monotony. Haydn is full of subtleties in this matter, which have frequently been mistaken for primitive features by people who fail to notice that they occur chiefly in Haydn's latest works. They would occur more often in Beethoven's but for the fact that the development of new resources must crowd out the use of subtleties in old resources that need elbow-room for their expression.

My tables on pp. 12–13 give you the extended key-relations. Use it as I would use the thriller's map of the scene of the crime. It is your security that the author has worked out his problem, and that you can work it out after him if you like. I do not call them Beethoven's key-relations, because they are already manifest in the works of Domenico Scarlatti, the son of Alessandro Scarlatti, who founded the whole system of classical tonality, and who in so doing went a considerable way in experimenting with them himself. The darker colours, such as A flat to C (VI to I) are often evident in Mozart, especially as purple patches during the second group in his expositions. The bolder and brighter key-relations, such as C major to E major (I to III), are explored to their limits by Haydn in his later works; but what no master did before Beethoven was to map out the new countries. With Domenico Scarlatti, they are *Arabian Night* marvels. Messrs. Thomas Cook may use a magic carpet as a pictorial advertisement, but the inventor of the magic carpet is not entitled to the credit for Messrs. Cook's organization.

Haydn and Mozart knew very well where the remoter key regions lay, but their practice, except in Mozart's above-mentioned purple passages, is to put the mutually remote keys side by side as the keys of complete sections: for instance, the key of a slow movement of a work; or, more intimately, the key of the trio of a minuet. Neither Haydn nor Mozart took the risk of giving a remote key an essential function in a continuous and highly organized movement. We must never forget that no key-relationship can be asserted by merely reaching a key in the course of various wanderings. You may safely ignore all commentators who find sensationally remote keys in the course of works by

Steibelt, Woelfl, and other fashionable worthies of Beethoven's day. Schubert is in quite another case. He was twenty-six years younger than Beethoven and died a year after him. He came only gradually under Beethoven's spell after his sense of tonality had developed quite independently; but his tonality is exactly Beethoven's in its fullest range, and is intensified by concentration in lyric forms to which Beethoven contributed little.

The best way to impress upon the reader the effects of Beethoven's extended tonality will be to disregard logical order and begin with the most vivid examples. A composer often has occasion to translate a theme from major to minor and vice versa. This may provide an acid test for his sense of values, for a composer may be as masterly as Mendelssohn by birth and education, and yet suffer from the professional delusion that things which look alike on paper remain unaffected by accidents of mode and tempo. I will not accuse Mendelssohn of blasphemies which he did not commit, but the reader will find it worth while to endure for a moment the shock that he will get if, when he knows the exquisite quiet pathos of the Finale of Beethoven's D minor Sonata, op. 31, no. 2, he will try the experiment of hearing it turned into D major. It is always easy, perhaps dangerously easy, to translate a passage from minor to major. Translation from major to minor is a fairly difficult exercise, and when Mozart writes a big movement in a minor key with a second group in the mediant (so-called relative major) major, the ways in which he later on recapitulates it in the tonic minor are by no means literal translations and are consummate achievements in the pathetic style.

Now take one of those openings of a major movement that proceed a step upwards to the supertonic—as in the principal theme of the first movement of the First Symphony (Ex. 9, opposite). What would become of such openings if we translated them into the minor? There is no supertonic key related to the minor. We have to reckon backwards and take the major flat seventh, to which our minor key is supertonic; but the whole point of our opening is that it is a step up which by no reasonable interpretation can become a step down. A step up it must therefore be, and we do not want to represent our supertonic chord by an imperfect triad which can be nothing but a feebly evasive expression of the dominant.

Now look at Beethoven's glorious and profound answer to this riddle at the beginning of the *Sonata Appassionata*, op. 57, to show the development of Beethoven's style in one of three allied but contrasted examples. You will find this flat supertonic in my table under the head of Neapolitan relations, a name which I have chosen because its origin is in a highly coloured chord known as the Neapolitan sixth which occurs as ante-penultimate in some

cadences both in major and minor keys. You will have no difficulty in identifying the chord as used in the Finale of the C sharp
minor Sonata commonly called the 'Moonlight'.

In the *Sonata Appassionata*, the opening phrase is so impressive
that exact translation into the flat supertonic can only add to its
impressiveness. Afterwards Beethoven needs eight bars of home
dominant to establish his home tonic firmly.

Ex. 9

Two years after the *Sonata Appassionata*, Beethoven used the
flat supertonic in the same way in the second Rasoumovsky
Quartet (E minor, op. 59, no. 2). Fétis, the learned compiler of
the *Biographie Universelle des Musiciens*, who said of Wagner that
'this music of the future is already that of the past', cites this
opening as an example of unsurpassable banality. Such criticisms
arise from inability to separate essentials from accidents. A dance-
band will play a succession of dances in keys the effect of which
in juxtaposition must be simply ignored by any one with an ear
sensitive to key-relations; and many singing-masters will support
their pupils' exercises with triads mounting by semitones in crass
disregard of grammar. Fétis obviously heard nothing better in
Beethoven's grandest modulations than their superficial resemblance to such accidents. 'A primrose by the river's brim'
was not even a yellow primrose to him. It was as a blot of yellow
to the eyes of a man whose experience associates the colour with

the debris of objects thrown at unpopular political candidates. Now, if you really want to turn the opening of the E minor Quartet into a banality, all you need do is to repeat the initial two loud chords on the flat supertonic, as well as the quiet phrase that follows the bar of silence. Though Beethoven's chords become mysterious by standing rhythmically on the edge of a void, and though their challenge is dramatic, they do assert the tonic and dominant as a formula quite detached from the intensely personal theme that follows. The theme of the *Sonata Appassionata* is personal from its very first note, and as such bears repetition. The formula does not. In the E minor Quartet you will find that Beethoven has to establish his E minor after that flat supertonic by several bars of dominant, exactly as in the *Sonata Appassionata*.

Now take the opening of one of Beethoven's most highly concentrated works, perhaps the first in which features of his 'third manner' may be suspected. Here is the opening of the F minor Quartet, op. 95:

Ex. 10

It is violent, both in its two bars of tonic theme and in its three bars of rhythms prancing around the dominant. Neither of these angry utterances is a formula. But try the effect of repeating these five bars a semitone higher on the flat supertonic, and you will be horrified at the banality. Your horror will be worth while if it enhances your sense of the pathos of Beethoven's reply, in which the violoncello, beginning the first phrase with violence, is rebuked by the melting harmonies which enter above it. There is a subtlety in these harmonies with which I shall deal later. Throughout our survey of Beethoven, it will be convenient often to return to this F minor Quartet, which would be the complete quintessence of Beethoven, if it were not, as Beethoven once expressly entitled it, a '*quartetto serioso*'.

The flat supertonic is hardly an indirect key-relation at all, for its chord is the inevitable result of making the lower half of the minor scale correspond with the upper, a point which will become more significant if we think of the scale as downwards instead of upwards. Hungarian music shows a decided fondness for a mixed major and minor scale which descends thus: C, B natural, A flat, G; answered by F, E natural, D flat, C. Every minor scale has

Ex. 11

a flat sixth, which tends to fall upon the major dominant chord. Why not, then, answer your flat sixth by a flat supertonic, which has a similar tendency to fall upon a major tonic chord? Neither the dominant nor the tonic is compelled to be major. The minor mode is an elastic affair in which the dominant chord is by no means compelled to be major, except in actual full closes; and, accordingly, the flat supertonic can quite as well be followed by a minor tonic. It thus deepens the pathetic possibilities and ironies of the minor mode. But, from its analogy with a chord that impinges on the necessarily major dominant chord, it becomes equally capable of entering into relations with a major tonic.

Text-books on harmony are still all too persistent in regarding modulations to keys a semitone apart as extremely remote. But we must not be misled by the typographical accidents that such modulations often need a bristling array of sharps and flats to express them; besides which, it is often more convenient to write the second of the keys as its enharmonic double, which will mean the same notes upon the pianoforte, but which will theoretically imply a key that is not related at all. For instance, later on in the first movement of the F minor Quartet, Beethoven, being firmly established in D flat, twice has a fierce outburst upon its flat supertonic, which, for practical purposes, he writes as the key of D natural. If he were a pedant who would not trust good musicians to play in tune without diverting their attention from music to a course of ear-training in the appreciation of mathematical minutiae, beyond the range of accuracy of human fingers on actual fiddle-strings and finger-boards, he would have comforted theorists by writing in the scale of E double flat. Even then, this would not have done much good to harmonic theorists who still persist in treating harmony and tonality independently of musical form, and who have not yet realized the elementary fact that the great composers make their meaning recognizable either by direct juxtaposition or by a strong appeal to the listener's memory.

Beethoven's other remote key-relations need not be described in detail. The difficulty of describing the ordinary direct key-relations lies in the fact that they are the simplest, as well as the most important, things in harmony, and therefore do not attract more attention in themselves than that vital difference between the nominative and accusative which enables us to tell who killed whom. The remoter key-relations always have directly impressive effects when used by a master who does not squander them. No amount of squandering by later masters or of crowding out by later resources can alter their value in their proper place. Beethoven had penetrated to the root of the matter before he was fifteen. One of the most important passages in the C major Sonata, op. 2, no. 3 (first movement, bars 25–45), is based on a passage that occurs in one of three juvenile quartets. The *Bagatelles*, op. 33, were published in 1802, and Beethoven had certainly by that time polished them to perfection. It is, therefore, unfortunate for their reputation that the autograph bears, in a scrawl indistinguishable from Beethoven's, the date 1783. At that date Beethoven could never have come within dreaming distance of their style, all the more because they are exactly the bagatelles that he calls them; but the underlying ideas very probably did date from 1783. They are full of precisely the kind of wit and fancy that children can originate and enjoy, and that men of genius can retain throughout their lives. One of the wittiest is No. 3, which begins with as straightforward a line as 'Three children sliding on the ice'. For convenience I will quote Beethoven's first couplet as it is *not*.

Ex. 12

This is dull. Melodic modulations from a major tonic to its unchanged mediant or submediant have no very definite character. A modulation to the dominant would be commonplace, and therefore less dull to tastes who find dullness more dull when it is vague than when it is obvious; but the three children were sliding on the ice 'all on a summer's day'. Put sharps to all the F's in bars 5–7 and handle the 8th bar thus:

Ex. 13

and you at once have an authentic word of power from Beethoven.

Note the way in which Beethoven returns to his key. He shows how the summer's day originated. The F sharp merely changes to F natural, and so we find ourselves at home.

The critic who values a work of art according to the number of epigrams it contains will despise the rest of this *Bagatelle* for containing no other interesting harmonies at all, but the rest is exactly right. Beethoven's D major is not quite parallel to the 'all on a summer's day' of the rhyme, for the rhyme is meant to be nonsense, and is continued with similar contradictions to the bitter end; but Beethoven's bright flash of D major is perfectly sensible, and the rest of the *Bagatelle* very rightly shows no sense that anything shocking has happened.

Now take the opening of a very remarkable sonata, the *Sonata Quasi Una Fantasia*, op. 27, no. 1, twin-brother to the so-called 'Moonlight' Sonata. Bülow considered the first movement of this E flat Sonata unworthy of Beethoven; but, humorist as Bülow himself was, his formidable cleverness was not always a match for Beethoven's still more formidable skill in the cruel sport of prig-sticking. The French Revolution had shaken the foundations of aristocracy all over the world too thoroughly to allow the further musical development of Mozart's exquisite irony, though the Viennese aristocracy in its dealings with Beethoven showed not only the perfection of tact, but a generous admiration for his character which went far beyond mere tolerance of his fiery Republican outspokenness. It is worth while harking back some fifty years and being for a moment unfair to Lord Chesterfield in order to see what a hopelessly vulgar and Philistine figure he would present in contrast to such understanding of the moral, as well as the intellectual, values of genius. On the other hand, compared with Beethoven, Dr. Johnson had a right to consider himself, as he once said, 'a very polite man'. At all events, he was a good listener; and, if he often lost his temper in argument, he at least recognized it as a positive advantage that in conversing with the king a man may not fly into a passion. Royalty was the last consideration that prevented Beethoven from flying into a passion, or even from rapping Archduke pupils, as well as commoners, over the knuckles for playing wrong notes; to which a certain peeress retorted by thumping him violently on the shoulders when, in playing his D minor Sonata, op. 31, no. 2, he became so excited (*temperamentvoll* is, I believe, the correct word) that his rendering of bars 52–54 sounded as if he were merely dusting the keys. Where there is this amount of give-and-take between artists and their patrons, the finer social reciprocities of wit will not be absent. If Beethoven as a master of irony is less dangerous than Mozart, that is only because we know Beethoven to be a master of tragedy and are therefore less liable to fall into the mistake, so admirably defined by Edward Fitzgerald when, in the intervals of polishing his *Omar Khayyám*, he said that 'people will not believe Mozart to be powerful because he is so beautiful'. It would be idle to pretend that the beginning of op. 27, no. 1, is powerful. Persons who find it childish may be rebuked with the correction that it is childlike. If, on the other hand, any one should plead that the first eight bars are in double counterpoint which is afterwards inverted in bars 67–70 and 75–78, and that this is a highly intellectual procedure, Beethoven himself would uproariously laugh the belief out of court. The real intellectual values of this ostentatiously ridiculous movement depend on the following facts.

The opening nursery rhyme, with its bass, or, to speak learnedly, its counterpoint, running like a kitten in pursuit of its tail, has nothing but the most ordinary harmonies of the key of E flat. It has not even a half-close on the dominant. Its cadences are tonic, and so is that of the very sentimental new four-bar strain that follows without change of key; but this new strain, like the first one, needs a second strain, and the second strain begins with a bright chord of C major. As a mere point of colour, the effect is exactly that of the D major already quoted in the F major *Bagatelle*. But the chord does not turn out to be a key at all, but is mere leading-note to our next-door neighbour, the supertonic, and the tune, having left its message next door, finishes itself at home as if nothing had happened. Nothing, in fact, has happened. Further, after this burst of energy, the first tune returns in both its strains with their repeats. The repeats are varied by the following highly intellectual process. The original rhythm being *Dum-dum-dum*, the variation is at first *Dum-dum-dum-dum-dum*, which, in the repetition of the second strain is, however, developed into *Diddle-diddle-diddle-diddle-dum*; after which, something really does happen. An energetic movement begins in the key of C major. There is no process of modulating to C major. There need not be. We have already heard its chord explained away as mere leading-note to the supertonic. The only novelty is that we are now transported to the real key of C major, existing in its own right. This episode is worked out as a complete symmetrical section, but the repetition of its second strain diverts the harmony through C minor to the home dominant of E flat. The passing through C minor establishes the indirect relation of C major to E flat, and, by dwelling on the home dominant, Beethoven makes us take the return to E flat seriously as a reasoned process and not as a mere juxtaposition. The final *da capo* of the opening theme is only slightly more intellectual with its double counterpoint than the former rhythmic variation. Then, with an appropriate touch of the subdominant, hitherto unheard, there is a line of coda which, if played simply and gravely enough, with a sense of beauty in pianoforte tone, faintly hints at more serious things. And the rest of the sonata has an energy which deserves to be called powerful as well as serious.

Any novel-reader whose tastes are not bounded by the average best-seller will understand that a witty writer must be careful neither to make his characters talk too cleverly for their place in his world, nor to fall into the trick of abusing his own creative authority by bullying them. There is no doubt that the first movement of opus 27, no. 1, is 'fooling'. Tastes may differ whether the fooling is excellent or not, but there is no fooling in the handling of that chord of C major, first as an illusion that fades into the common light of the home supertonic, and, secondly, as a key in its own right; and there is no fooling in the rest of the sonata. Probably we shall be wise to be not less unkind than our gruff and grim Beethoven to such aristocratic fooling. I have already mentioned my violent objection to a type of examination question which requires the candidate to modulate through a series of keys. My own answers to such questions would probably shock the setters of them by modulating in many cases just as Beethoven does when he wishes the new key to produce its full effect; that is to say, by not modulating at all.

Another of these cases of major submediant from a major tonic occurs in the Prisoners' Chorus in *Fidelio*. The prisoners have, contrary to the orders of the governor, been let out of their cells and allowed to walk in the garden. Beethoven did not know how to bully his librettist, and after several revisions the libretto of *Fidelio* remained a hindrance to him, even in its final form; but he was a master of stage-timing where the libretto permitted, and the entry of the prisoners is of an overpowering pathos, achieved by the simplest means. The key of B flat is straightforwardly established, in a few slow chords arising from a deep bass; and when all the prisoners are assembled, they sing, at first in hushed voices, a pathetic strain of joy at seeing daylight and breathing fresh air; but the highest pathos is reached when one of them, with a sudden hope of real release, begins a new melody in G major. To have modulated from B flat to G would have been as infuriating as to preach to the prisoners a sermon on the blessings of liberty. The proper occasion for modulations is very different. The prisoners see that they are watched by a sentry, and they whisper to each other to speak softly and keep carefully within bounds. For this counsel, modulations are appropriate, and the more obscure the better. Beethoven deliberately avoids establishing any sense of key until, having landed on what happens to be a chord of D major, evidently in the sense of a dominant, he drops from it, not to G major, but back to B flat, and there resumes the first strain of the chorus fortissimo; after which, with further apprehensive whispers that 'we are watched and must keep within bounds', the prisoners disperse into the garden.

When Beethoven wishes to give remoter keys important functions in the organization of continuous movements, these immediate juxtapositions will not be to the purpose, for their effect is to disjoin sections, not to emphasize continuity. It is true that the remoter keys establish themselves just because they are not directly related. You may dwell in a directly related key for a long time without becoming sure that it is not merely part of a melody that begins and ends in the tonic, and the only way to make the tonic sink out of sight is to harp upon the dominant of the new key with so much emphasis and accessory harmony that it becomes what I have called the enhanced dominant, such as is often mistakenly described as the major supertonic.

We have seen from the first incident in op. 27, no. 1, that one chord can no more make a remote key than one swallow can make a summer: the remote key must establish itself by displaying its own retinue of chords. But it can so establish itself without any preparation. It needs preparation only when we are to be convinced that it is not a detached episode but part of a continuous action. The dominant preparation—that is to say, preparation on its own dominant—remains the simplest and most obvious kind. If the composer is handling his new resources as paradoxes to be put forward in a provocative manner, he may establish his remote key in quite a short passage of dominant preparation. Thus, in the G major Sonata, op. 31, no. 1, twelve bars are all that he needs by way of dominant preparation from the first shock of the F major chord at the join of bar 53/54 until the

B major second group begins in bar 66. Most of the rest of the group, by the way, is in B minor, the ordinary mediant; but this does not wipe out the impression made by the B major of its eight-bar main theme.

The clearest of all lessons in the development of Beethoven's style can be obtained by comparing the G major Sonata, op. 31, no. 1, with the 'Waldstein' Sonata, op. 53, adding thereto the Andante in F, which at first belonged to the 'Waldstein' Sonata, but for excellent reasons was extruded from it and published separately. In the 'Waldstein' Sonata, Beethoven's wider range of key is no longer either a paradox or an affair to be confined to display in sections. Not only in the choice of the mediant major for the second group, but also in the bold harmonic lay-out of the opening, the 'Waldstein' Sonata develops the harmonic idea of opus 31, no. 1. Moreover, op. 31, no. 1, has a slow movement which is definitely reactionary in its florid elegance; and the sonata ends with a graceful and brilliant rondo of which the coda pauses, rather rhetorically, to reflect, with the fatal consequence that it bursts into a *fou rire* and ends the sonata as a joke. As with the first movement of op. 27, no. 1, tastes may differ whether the whole result is convincing. If you can really enjoy the company of that provocative young man, the first movement, for nearly seven minutes, you will need all your politeness to save yourself from a yawn while you give your attention for ten minutes to that dear old lady the Adagio grazioso, who would certainly dread the irruption into her drawing-room of the young man with his muddy boots. All the same, there is, as in op. 27, no. 1, good comedy in the contrast, though, on the small scale of sonata-time, ten minutes' restriction to grand-motherly company-manners is a high price to pay for it.

In the 'Waldstein' Sonata there is nothing provocative. The harmonic facts are now among the eternal musical verities, whether they are new or old; and though the sonata again included a reactionary slow movement which Beethoven wrote in its place, page numbers and all, and though this movement was much less reactionary and obviously much more beautiful than the Adagio of op. 31, no. 1, Beethoven soon discovered that there was no excuse for it, and that what the sonata really wanted in that place was no reaction but, on the contrary, a deeply emotional assertion of its new harmonic principles in their highest concentration. You have only to see how he modulates from F to D flat in bars 245–249 in the first movement, to say nothing of the miracle of bars 167–168 compared with bars 12–13, and you will see that when, in the Andante in F, Beethoven's chief purple patch is the modulation from F to D flat spaced out in the following emphatic way—

Ex.14

he is in the position of a writer who says, 'Then a strange thing
happened,' by way of introducing an event which is obviously
less strange than many things which he has already told with full
power and restraint of style.

A reference to my tables of key-relations will show that we
have not gone very far in the catalogue of what keys Beethoven
can bring into organic connexion; but once the listener can
recognize by ear the effects produced by such organization, he
need not burden his mind with minutiae. Certain very remote
keys can be brought into contact by changing both modes of the
relation, as is shown in the third level of my tables, the doubly
indirect keys. Hence the startling effect of the E major slow
movement of Beethoven's C minor Concerto, which so frightened
one eminent pianist that he used to extemporize an elegant
Chopinesque passage between the two movements in order to
explain it away. The converse relation is to be found in the
Sonata, op. 106, in B flat, to which the slow movement opposes
what is really the key of G flat minor, written, for practical reasons,
as F sharp minor; the connexion being B flat/B flat minor/G flat
(♭VI)/F sharp minor (♭vi). In the F minor Quartet, you will find
the slow movement (allegretto) is in D major (♯VI).

It now remains to describe certain important ways in which
Beethoven organizes his modulations. When he wishes to connect
two keys by something less crude than immediate juxtaposition,
one of his favourite ways is to take the tonic or dominant chord
of one key, knock away some of its notes, hold on to the remainder,
and then surround it with what will make the tonic or dominant
chord of a new key. But sometimes he does not wish to display
the connexion between the keys at all. It is a most vital distinction
in Beethoven's, as in all great music, whether the modulation
asserts a key-relation directly, explains it circumstantially, digresses
at large, or deliberately mystifies. Each of these four cases has
exactly the same importance in music that they obviously have
in literature. In illustrating and discriminating between them,
we shall have ample opportunity of pointing out the effects of all
the rest of the key-relations displayed in my tables.

WAYS AND MEANS: CAUSES AND SURPRISES

ONE of the most powerful passages in Beethoven's early works is that which begins the second group of the first movement of the A major Sonata, op. 2, no. 2. After sixteen very thoughtful bars of dominant preparation, the second group begins in the dominant minor at bar 58, and then, instead of illustrating that key, continues with a series of startling modulations which reach the extreme distance of B flat in their course before they restore any hope of a return to E minor. Yet this remote key of B flat is the merest incident in the whole passage, and you will not have completed the harmonic sense of Beethoven's device until you have reached bar 87, nor the rhythmic sense until you have added the supplementary four bars closing into bar 92. On the lines of the old-fashioned harmony-books the passage can be explained as a series of enharmonic modulations with details not uninteresting to those who care for such things. The explanation is correct as far as it goes. It is quite true that the D sharp in bar 60 really turns to E flat in bar 61, and the F sharp in bar 64 to G flat in bar 65; and it is even true that a violinist or a singer would, as soon as he knew the sense of the passage, instinctively mark these changes in the course of a *vibrato*, though Beethoven has not troubled to recognize them in his notation. Also, it is important to recognize that such enharmonic modulations, where they are genuine, do really mystify the listener, whether the instrument is a rigidly tempered affair like the pianoforte with all its distinctions ironed out into twelve equal semitones to the octave, or whether, like the human voice, the violin, and the slide-trombone, it makes its own intonation and can approach mathematical ideals to the limits of human muscular accuracy; and can, for the same human reason, go abominably out of tune. The only trouble about the grammatical explanation of these enharmonic affairs is, first, that for general readers, and also for experienced composers, grammar is a dull subject when the study of it does not happen to be a painful necessity; and secondly—a far more serious objection— that the grammatical sense of this passage could not only be kept inviolate, but made much clearer, by simple alterations in the bass that would literally knock the bottom out of the whole plot. If the reader can make the acquaintance of Haydn's delightful A major Quartet, op. 20, no. 6, he will find in much the same part of the movement a delightful discursive passage which, though it does not modulate to extreme distances, shows that there would be nothing new in Beethoven's indulging in discursive

modulations here; but Haydn is being discursive, and his movements from key to key, though charmingly capricious, are perfectly clear. Now in this passage of Beethoven's there are two
unprecedented facts: the first is that, at a cardinal point in the
exposition of a movement—that is to say, just where the composer
or dramatist must be careful that his discursive licence helps
instead of hindering him to display all his data to the listener—
Beethoven indulges in enharmonic modulations the very nature
of which makes it impossible for us to know where we are. How
can you trace a key-relation through a chord that has changed
its meaning before it resolves? Alice, when in Wonderland, may
have been very dull in not seeing for herself that one of the
masters in the Mock-Turtle's school was called Tortoise 'because
he taught us', but we are not all as clever as mock-turtles.

The second paradox about Beethoven's passage is that, after
all, it sounds anything but discursive and aimless. On the contrary, it is one of the most solid and cogent affairs of dramatic
destiny to be found in any music. And the secret is ridiculously
simple. It is that the bass is rising steadily by tones and semitones from E up to the F sharp a ninth above. At this point it
pauses with dramatic questionings, and the following eight bars
(4+4) complete the remaining steps to the dominant of E; for
it does not matter through what octaves you distribute the G sharp,
A, A sharp, and B; the harmonic sense of rising ignores the
octave, just as your ear will ignore a change of octave when a
soprano voice hands over the continuation of a melody to a bass
voice. Thus, a bass that gave the roots of the chords would
underline the grammar of the enharmonic marvels at the cost of
the whole dramatic sense; and this may show why musicians who
have large views of music are even more bored by the details of
harmonic analysis than amateurs who study musical grammar in
the hope of finding it interesting. A gradually rising bass produces
tension and excitement, if only because it is in the general case
of a rising voice. A gradually falling bass will obviously produce,
not necessarily 'that sinking feeling', but at all events a feeling
of relaxation, or drooping. At a point closely corresponding to
this wonderful passage in opus 2, no. 2, you will find in the
Sonata, op. 2, no. 3, a beautiful passage on such a falling bass
(first movement, bars 27–38). The modulations are not sensational, there is one notch in the course of the descent, and the
whole manner is a little nearer to the charming discursiveness of
the passage in Haydn's Quartet, op. 20, no. 6; but it is remarkable
as having been first written in a shorter form in one of the three
Pianoforte Quartets Beethoven composed at the age of fifteen,
and I do not know of anything in Haydn or Mozart that seriously
anticipates its principle. In one of Beethoven's profoundest

works, the Sonata, op. 81*a*, *Les Adieux, L'Absence, et Le Retour*, the introduction and first movement show, in spite of moments of energetic protest on a rising bass, the depression underlying the mood of two of the manliest of friends bidding each other farewell, for the bass is almost continually falling, sometimes in quick scales and sometimes in slow steps. Of course, we cannot suppose that so absurdly simple an affair as a rising or falling bass can have failed to happen, or even been avoided, in earlier music. The whole of Bach's E minor Prelude (Book I, no. 10, in the Forty-Eight) consists of two steady descents of its bass as soon as it has disposed of its four tonic and dominant chords before each descent; and the marvellous harmonies of the recitative at the end of the Chromatic Fantasia are supported on chords of which the bass slowly descends by semitones; but the descents in the E minor Prelude, though expressive enough, are a decorative device (I need not have said 'though', for, if decoration is not expressive, it is nothing). And when Bach's harmonies are marvels, as in the Chromatic Fantasia, his deliberate purpose is to astonish and bewilder. They are, in fact, like the harmonies of the 'Et exspecto' of the B minor Mass: assertions that faith is mere reason unless it can put its trust in mysteries.

Beethoven was mystical enough, but his use of the gradually rising or falling bass is neither decorative nor mysterious. Its purpose is to give the most solid dramatic reasons for modulations which would otherwise be mere accidents. In the Sonata, op. 2, no. 2, he has even shown that not only the utmost remoteness of key, but the deliberate concealment of such key-relationships as are present, can be perfectly reconciled with the duties of dramatic exposition. The development of the first movement of the *Sonata Appassionata* contains the most famous of the climaxes he achieves by this means. Being an incident in the course of development, it is not restrained by the conditions of an exposition. A full explanation of it must be part of an analysis of the whole first movement, and for that there is no room in the present volume; so I must refer the reader to my *Companion to Beethoven's Pianoforte Sonatas*, published by the Associated Board of the Royal Schools of Music. The passage in question is that which leads to the recapitulation (bars 109–135). The essential points are as follows.

The calm theme with which it begins had first appeared in the exposition in A flat (bars 35/36–39) as a four-bar melody on a bass which happens to rise simply because an orderly rising bass is here in good style, whereas a bass of root-notes would be clumsy. In the exposition, the entry of the theme has been prepared by a very long passage of dominant preparation. Its appearance in the development in D flat is still more impressive, because

Beethoven has taken the extraordinary risk of arresting his action
by not only reproducing his whole passage of dominant preparation
on the threshold of this D flat, but by actually adding four more
bars to it, bars for which he is obliged to invent entirely new
matter, since the original preparation had purposely contained
very little matter at all, being of the nature of long-drawn sighs
and gasps ending in exhaustion.

Incidentally, these four extra bars (105–108) should convince
the reader that it is folly to rely upon the derivations of themes
as evidences that the music is logically constructed. The classics
of music may not be infallible, but they cannot be so foolish as
a criterion of musical logic according to which the *Sonata
Appassionata* is illogical.

The calm theme, having thus entered with enhanced impressiveness in D flat, should after four bars begin to repeat itself in the
upper octave. Instead of this, the bass continues rising. This
forces the theme in a crescendo through a series of keys which
it is not worth while specifying. The point is: first, that the bass
rises for two octaves, and that at the top of its climb articulate
music ceases. So far, we may hope that the driest of grammarians,
once he has been convinced that harmonies on a gradually rising
bass are not aesthetically replaceable by harmonies in root posi-
tions, will have seen the point of this tremendous climax. Yet
there are commentators who follow a correct description of the
rise of two octaves by enthusiastic admiration of its sequel in the
Jacob's-ladder steps of nine bars of a diminished seventh, rising
for another two octaves and descending for four octaves. They
do not improve matters when they tell us that the arpeggios
are brilliant. What is your appreciation of Hamlet's soliloquy
worth if your highest enthusiasm is expressed in the statement
contained in the line 'Ay, there's the rub'? Beethoven, like many
Germans of his and of later days, knew his Shakespeare remarkably
well, at all events in very good translations. His rising bass is the
hysterica passio to which Lear, already dreading the approach of
madness, cries 'Down!' Its climax is inarticulate. Melody
disappears and harmony becomes ambiguous, for the diminished
seventh, though it implies a dominant, happens to omit the dominant from its notes, and is notoriously ready to shift its intonation
and imply any of three other widely remote dominants, as we
already saw in that wonderful passage in opus 2, no. 2. Rhythm
itself would disappear but for the fact that, so long as we remain
conscious, we cannot get rid of time. In the present passage,
the first sign of a return to articulate speech is in an ominous
rhythmic figure (bar 120), and the diminished seventh resolves
into the home dominant, and so leads us to the recapitulation.

The more we study Beethoven's harmonic devices, the more

inseparable we shall find them from his rhythmic proportions and his dramatic purposes. The reasoned observation of a clever and otherwise appreciative critic, that Beethoven has of all great composers contributed least to the development of harmony, thus shows that that critic, in common with most harmonic theorists, has never considered harmony on a large scale at all. To great composers, music is neither a game nor a science, but a language, and great masters of language, though they create much actual new language, do so mainly by setting up a powerful association of their new ideas with old words, and contribute very little by way of actual new coinages, and still less by the portmanteau process which Humpty Dumpty elucidated when he construed the first stanza of *Jabberwocky*.

In the course of our investigation, we are sure to come upon illustrations of the extraordinary harmonic results Beethoven achieves by sheer concentration and overlapping of thought. Such results are genuine harmonic extensions, not new theories. They are like the harmonic audacities of Bach, who is quite rightly regarded as the greatest master of harmony the world has ever seen, but who, in all probability, did not produce a single audacity that had not been anticipated by older composers. As Bach happened to work often in small forms, where it was very desirable to concentrate upon harmonic details, he was able to produce several hundred glorious settings of plain chorale tunes, and it has been remarked that if Mozart or Beethoven had attempted a similar collection it would hardly have been worth looking at. This may be true, but what is much more certain is that, if Mozart or Beethoven had been foolish enough to make any such attempt, and had persisted long enough to accumulate a large volume, they must have taken immense pains and devoted all that energy and time to the resulting failure, instead of producing a much larger bulk of the masterpieces which we now possess. All Beethoven's great harmonic discoveries are long-distance effects, and in these his range is unsurpassed by Wagner, though Wagner's elbow-room is the whole four days of his *Ring* tetralogy, whereas Beethoven's is the quarter of an hour of the largest possible movement in sonata style. Miracles will not extend the range of harmony, any more than magic carpets will anticipate the aeroplane. But second-rate art often depends upon marvels which will not long remain marvellous, and so condemns itself to lose effect quite apart from those changes of fashion from which the greatest art is not immune. In illustrating the ways in which Beethoven has enlarged the range of key-relation, we have seen that while his discoveries are new to him, his manner is apt to be provocative and paradoxical, and that he abandons this manner as soon as his discoveries are no longer paradoxes to him. But it would be a mistake to infer from this that familiarity has made the discoveries less effective either to him or to his posterity. The paradoxical manner is permanently in character with the comedy of opus 31, no. 1. The music is not talking about a harmonic world in which remoter key-relationships are commonplace. The fact that we travel in motors and aeroplanes nowadays does not make us less amused at the dignity of the Royal coachman who insisted on travelling on the engine-plate of the first Royal railway-train.

I have more than once referred to Bach's use of enharmonic and otherwise remote modulations for the purpose of astonishing and bewildering. How is it that they still astonish and bewilder, although Beethoven has rationalized the whole possible range of tonality? I know nothing more impressive in the aesthetics of music than the fact that Bach's modulations never include any portion of the region that lies between the direct key-relation and the extreme distances beyond the pale. The direct key-relations he treats as the horses of the Red and White Knights treat their riders, whom they let get on and off as if they were tables. Bach will not be hindered by pedantic scruples from drifting beyond the range, and, when he does so drift, he will not make any effort to assert a non-existent key-relation; but it is surely a vitally important fact that all his bolder modulations lead actually to regions which remain remote so long as the conception of tonality has meaning at all. It is a commonplace of criticism to say that the chord of the diminished seventh, which Weber uses to such excellent purpose for gruesome effects in *Der Freischütz*, can no longer thrill us. This is true only of composers whose familiarity with it has that second-hand quality that breeds contempt. Weber is no Beethoven, but his genius is of a high order, and the real difficulty of a modern production of *Der Freischütz* does not come from anything outworn in the music. The music depends upon the libretto; and the trouble is that the libretto, in spite of considerable merits as such, is not literature. There is no difficulty in appreciating Weber's simple and admirable expressions of romantic and superstitious horror if stage-managers and producers can find an artistic solution of the problem of supporting these in the staging of a libretto which combines the earnestness of a moral tale with the bogy tricks of a pantomime. If the librettist had been such a poet as Weber, our own superiority to German forest demonology would do no more harm to *Der Freischütz* than the superior social philosophy of Bernard Shaw can do to the poetry of Shakespeare. The criticism of works of art can never be correct until we see each artistic resource as it is in its own context. This presents no more difficulty, and needs no more historical or technical knowledge, than the ability to see whether a novelist is imputing to any of his characters an utterance which is too stupid or too clever for the person he has so far succeeded in presenting to us. When he brings into his imaginary world a hitherto unprecedented range of ideas, his difficult and dangerous task will consist in convincing us that the ideas do belong to his world. Nothing is easier than for the author to expound his ideas while he stands outside his work and preaches. He can even save a little time by turning his characters into his own mouthpiece, regardless of any other reason for their existence. The way of the highest art is to make a coherent world of which the creator is like Mother Carey in Kingsley's *Water Babies*, who has achieved the art of sitting still and making things make themselves. In the extrusion of the Andante in F from the 'Waldstein' Sonata, we have seen what I believe is the only evidence of Beethoven's difficulty in fusing the elements of his new harmonic world. We have now to consider how from first to last his modulations retain their power to be marvellous. Here, again, I will begin with the most startling effects.

Any one who inflicts upon himself the study of my tables of tonality will be surprised to find that the changes of supertonic from major to minor are deported from their obvious place in the second line and placed beyond the pale under the title, the best that I can find, of 'contradictory' keys. It is an undoubted fact that only in the most banal of dance music or in parodistic imitation of its effects will you find C major and D major in immediate juxtaposition. There are more reasons for this than we have time fully to explore here, but we may be satisfied with the obvious reason, namely, that it is very difficult, if not impossible, to convince the listener that the key of the major supertonic is a new key at all. Its chords occur so normally as those of a mere enhanced dominant that to treat it as anything else produces, even to an unsophisticated ear, an effect of downright ignorance. Take our first illustration—the transition in the first movement of the G major Sonata, op. 14, no. 2—and see how you like the effect of following bar 25 by a theme in A major beginning thus:

Ex. 15

Remember that in all such experiments you must begin your alternative versions from the beginning of the movement.

Apart from the accidental juxtapositions of restaurant music, it is only in very special circumstances that we can feel the major supertonic to be a real key at all; and, where we can feel this, the effect will be very astonishing, unless, of course, it is mere non-sense. If you wish to understand Beethoven, one of the things that must remain deeply rooted in your musical consciousness is the opening of the 'Eroica' Symphony, with its marvellous results in the recapitulation. Up to a certain point, the theme consists entirely of the chord of E flat, which is the home tonic; but at its fifth bar (bar 7 of the whole movement) a cloud comes over the tonality in the shape of a mysterious C sharp. This explains itself away. Now, when anything in Beethoven has entered and apparently merely explained itself away, we shall probably find that it will some day explain itself to very different purpose. The first movement of the 'Eroica' Symphony is the longest movement that Beethoven ever wrote, with the exception of the E flat Concerto, op. 73, which the wrathful republican ghost of Beethoven forbids me to call by its popular English title of the 'Emperor' Concerto, though Beethoven did, in fact, dedicate it to a Royal archduke for whom he had a deep affection. The second group of the *Eroica* is an enormous affair, containing a cloud of themes which completely stultify the English technical term 'second subject'; and these are not enough for the purposes of the still more enormous development, which contains an important and entirely new episodic theme in the remotest keys outside the pale. (Beethoven could have done what Schubert afterwards did, that is, shown a connexion between the minor flat supertonic as an indirect Neapolitan relation to his tonic, but nothing short of immediate cadential juxtaposition could make such an idea conceivable.)

The preparations for the return to the home tonic are on as huge a scale as the rest, and the tension of hushed expectancy becomes at last so great that, while the faint remains of a dominant chord are vibrating in the air, a horn prematurely brings in the first theme with its tonic notes. Even to-day, some people still make a ridiculous fuss about the harshness of this discord, apparently in the belief, not only that its context makes no difference to it, but that it could not offend their refined ears more if it were played on the most uncontrollably loud harmonium with the expression-stop out. Beethoven boxed the ears of one of his best friends who at a rehearsal exclaimed that the horn-player had come in wrong, and this discord is one of the best illustrations of the fact that all Beethoven's harmonic devices depend for their very grammar upon their place in a highly organized and extended scheme. But this discord is not yet the most important feature of Beethoven's return to his main theme.

When he comes to the C sharp which cast a cloud over the tonality, this note resolves downwards instead of upwards. In other words, it has become D flat. Do not imagine that this change is inexpressible on the pianoforte. The ear judges by sense, and all the experiments of modern composers in quarter-tones and other strange minutiae will not permanently deprive even the most experimental human ear of its capacity to ally itself with human reason. Now when this D flat has resolved downwards, it takes us inevitably into the key of F, which Beethoven chooses to represent as F major. There is no explaining this away as an enhanced dominant. This is not how enhanced dominants ever happen. At the beginning of the movement, the C sharp was a temporary cloud. It is now a dramatic event, and by changing into D flat has certainly disguised whatever key-relation may have followed it. A horn in F continues happily with the theme, which seems perfectly at ease in its strange position. The F becomes F minor, not with the belated and impracticable purpose of explaining itself away as the respectable supertonic of E flat, but in order to drop a major third down to its own flat submediant, D flat. It is a fact that D flat is the flat seventh, and has from E flat the exactly opposite effect to that of the major supertonic. Like its 'opposite number', it has always failed to qualify as an indirect relation. The openings of the G major Sonata, op. 31, no. 1, and of the 'Waldstein' Sonata prove, like many other bold openings of the type, that it is merely an enhanced subdominant. In analysing music, as distinguished from listening to it, we must not be more rash than Beethoven in arrogating to ourselves a capacity to recognize key-relations across a long distance without collateral evidence; but here there is no reasonable doubt that, after all the excitements of the return to the recapitulation, we do refer this blazing F major and dark D flat major to our home tonic, though, of course, we could make wild nonsense of the whole passage by substituting new themes. One thing is needed to restore the balance, and that is the home dominant, which in the whole of this process we have not heard at all since the first theme made its real entry. Accordingly, the D flat drops down another third and lands us on B flat, which is the home dominant; so the theme swarms up again from this bass and leads in four bars to a tutti which is safe at home.

The blazing effect of a major supertonic which cannot be explained away as an enhanced dominant is shown very dramatically on a melodic scale in the last variation of the Andante of the Trio in B flat, op. 97. Here, again, nothing can be learnt by taking the passage out of its context. We must have heard the sublime melody with its repeats and its penultimate climax on the subdominant, and we must have heard the four complete variations on the plan of *doubles*—that is to say, of increasing sub-divisions of rhythm—until in the fourth variation the tempo has to become slower to make room for the notes, and, when the theme returns at its original pace without any ornamentation, we must be enjoying as a novelty its pathetic new harmonies, which construe part of it as in keys related to its tonic minor. Only then shall we see the dramatic force of the query to which these harmonies lead, as if by accident, in its twelfth bar. The query is twice repeated, and its incredible answer is an outburst of the supreme climax in E major (II). As this is indeed incredible, the final cadence halts and is repeated with differences, eventually passing through a deep shadow, which happens to be the dominant chord of C major, again, as in the *Eroica* Symphony, the opposite number. As the whole procedure is, after all, only on a melodic scale, it is enough for this chord to explain itself away enharmonically, and so to pass by easy harmonies into the home tonic.

It is surely now clear that the effect of Beethoven's harmonic power cannot be weakened by later composers, who make a merely self-indulgent use of chords which are powerful in Beethoven, but which our reformers of Church music are now anxiously weeding out of our hymn-books. Words that are misused by bad writers do not mean the same thing as they mean in the vocabulary of great writers. The Fiend Huntsman's diminished seventh in *Der Freischütz* has not lost its effect, though the stage-producer may have his difficulties in raising the necromantic horrors of the Wolf's Glen to the height of Weber's music. Weber is and remains a born tone-poet, though, with all his genius for music-drama, he did not live to become either a learned composer or the master of a powerful style; but with Beethoven it is obviously ridiculous to trouble our heads about his mere harmonic vocabulary at all. These passages which I have found so difficult to describe are all grammatically cases of the diminished seventh, and to praise Beethoven for his masterly use of that chord is no better than to praise the ancient oracles, as reported by Latin poets and historians, for their masterly use of the accusative with infinitive. What matters is not the grammatical construction, but the dramatic results. When Beethoven's drama does happen to produce, or be produced by, something outside the range of harmony-books, as in that famous premature entry of the horn, or in the overlapping farewells at the end of *Les Adieux*, some of our most modern theorists remain hardly less shocked than Beethoven's most pedantic contemporaries.

Earlier composers, some great, some merely archaic, have occasionally anticipated the harmonic resource by which Wagner enlarged the bounds of music beyond Beethoven's scope—a device which the ostentatiously revolutionary Berlioz hated so violently, not only in Wagner but in earlier music, that, if Cherubini had been rash enough to grant Berlioz's request to be appointed Professor of Harmony, French academic music would to this day have been condemned to live upon fundamental basses and the weary, uneasy organist's hunt for the Lost Chord. Wagner's device consists in approaching an *appoggiatura* from an unexpected quarter and holding it so long that it gives rise to a chord that seems to be in an incredibly remote key. The *appoggiatura* then quietly resolves into the note on which it was leaning, and that note turns out to be a normal part of a real key. Such Wagnerian effects are almost the only ones which people who look for novelties in harmony are trained to recognize. A composer has advanced if he uses them ten times where Wagner used them once. If he does not use them at all, then he must invent some new theory in which all classical progressions are forbidden. Wagner's chromatic harmonies produce their effect at the moment; and as Wagner is a composer on the largest possible scale, they also have their long-distance results, like Beethoven's normalities. The strange chord at the beginning of the prelude to *Tristan* has three dramatic changes of meaning: first, shortly before the rise of the curtain; secondly, at the death of Tristan, when, as the symbol of love, it arises out of the theme of death; and thirdly, at the close of the whole work. Thus, Wagner's most characteristic resources prove in his hands to be as capable of long-distance connexions as Beethoven's. To Beethoven, they would have been as disturbing as they were to Berlioz.

It is very seldom that a composer or writer can simultaneously concentrate his energies on the working out of a new language and on the construction of big designs; but while it is thus hardly strange that Beethoven did not anticipate Wagner in a harmonic tendency which as far as we can see would obviously have confused his outlines, it is strange that neither Wagner nor any other composer seems to have followed up one of Beethoven's profoundest harmonic thoughts, unless we count one decidedly indigestible early experiment, in a detail of Wagner's *Flying Dutchman*, which some diligent critic might quote against me. This device is an extreme development of Beethoven's characteristic way of putting two keys together by cutting away part of a chord and replacing it by notes which transform the remainder into a new key. Beethoven sometimes presents us with a single note, or a fragment of unsupported melody, which he gives out just slowly enough to make us wonder what its key is to be. The most wonderful of all passages on this principle is to be found in the development of *Les Adieux* (Allegro, bars 57–74), where the fragments of the 'farewell' figure descend without accompaniment and find themselves in an incalculably remote new key at each step, the crowning surprise being that the eventual drift is towards the home tonic. Again, in the first movement of the E minor Sonata, op. 90 (bars 37–44), the scale of B flat reduces to a minimum the sense that we are on the flat supertonic of A minor, and when the B flat turns to A sharp, the notes that are built upon it are very shy and tactful to break to us the news that they are the diminished seventh in B minor.

But sometimes no explanation is forthcoming at the moment. It is not even recognizable as the 'cloud no bigger than a man's hand' that eventually covers the sky and brings the rainstorm. It is more like a mysterious speck seen by a person who has never heard of aeroplanes and cannot imagine what that object can be which is evidently so far off that to be visible at all it must be larger than any conceivable bird. At the beginning of the Violin Concerto, the second phrase introduces a mysterious D sharp in the all-pervading rhythm previously announced by the drums. The chords which follow this mysterious note resolve it correctly enough on the dominant as far as key is concerned, but they take a position which, evidently of set purpose, avoids resolving the mysterious note melodically. Later on (bars 65–70), the D sharp appears as part of a fully harmonized melody and sweetly explains itself away.

Perhaps the most drastic case of the kind is the C sharp which bursts in so savagely upon the conspiratorial laughter of the first theme of the Finale of Beethoven's Eighth Symphony (bar 17). This violent note is a stranger to the audience, but seems no stranger to the orchestra, who greet it with cheerful uproar. After the Finale has gone through many adventures and the first theme has returned with the apparent purpose of making itself comfortable in a quiet coda, this strange note bursts in again as D flat, and insists upon being taken seriously as a key-note under the title of D flat (♭VI). When doubt is cast upon this claim, the note becomes very angry and insists on being the dominant of an incredibly remote F sharp minor. From this a return to the tonic is attained only through strong representation, which perhaps, by a stretch of courtesy, we may call diplomatic.

These illustrations of Beethoven's long-distance harmonic effects must suffice. The refinements of detail in his harmonic style are infinite, and much harder to describe than those of Bach; especially as they are for the most part achieved on very familiar material. The searcher for colour effects will miss them, and the old-fashioned grammarians will either miss them or mistake them for grammatical blunders. They are, for the most part, the results of great compression of thought. When the simple but active mind of the Irish peasant combines two unrelated ideas in one expression, the offspring is known as a 'bull'. Great poets can

overawe us into taking mixed metaphors seriously. No one laughs
at Shakespeare for making Hamlet talk of 'taking up arms against
a sea of troubles', nor at the wrathful Milton for describing the
clergy as 'blind mouths'. One of Beethoven's profoundest works
is the Trio in E flat, op. 70, no. 2, and one of the duller futilities
of criticism is that which accuses its style of a relapse into Mozartean phraseology. Here is one of its most Mozartean phrases:

Ex. 16

Violin

Violoncello

Pianoforte

and, if any survivor of the method of teaching harmony by
describing the roots of chords thinks he can treat these progressions as chords in themselves, he is welcome to make the attempt.
In *Madam How and Lady Why*, Charles Kingsley pointed out
that chemical analysis might work for ever at the contents of
a plum-pudding without any chance of arriving at the essential
fact that the cook had boiled it in a cloth. What has happened
in this suavely Mozartean utterance of Beethoven's is that he
has compressed into two bars what could not have been said in
less than four if the bass had not taken upon itself to move faster
than the treble and so give a more than double meaning to the
melody.

RHYTHM AND MOVEMENT

QUITE unmusical people have been known to say that what they enjoy in music is rhythm. It is easy to make fun of these people by taking a military march or a waltz and gradually eliminating, by distance or other means, first the harmony, then the melody, until nothing is left but the big drum and, in the case of dance-music, the swinging tonics and dominants of the basses. Thus distance lends enchantment to the music; but, manifest as is the pleasure of the rhythm-lover at the gradual disappearance of melody and harmony, it does not compare with the beatific smile which would illuminate his face if the sounds were to approach him in the reverse order, beginning with the big drum and proceeding to the swing of the dance bass. Now, such innocent eurhythmists have the root of a matter about which many more instructed music-lovers are confused. Musical rhythm in the sixteenth century was not measurable by the big drum. It was very different from what it is to the modern lover of classical music, and its origins in medieval art-music were still more different. But Palestrina's rhythm, though avowedly measurable by the human pulse, retains the elasticity of speech-rhythm, even to the extent of being, like the Latin and Romance languages to which it was sung, much more an affair of quantity than of accent. Only recently has our musical culture begun to recover and inculcate a sense of the rhythmic freedom of Palestrina and the madrigalists; and the recovery of this sense is delayed by our own habits of hard rhythmic accentuation, which we persist in attaching to sixteenth-century music in the sense of violent displacings of accent. We cannot without practice return to the habit of merely counting our beats and letting the accents slide as easily and smoothly as the words demand.

Such aspects of rhythm I shall call speech-rhythm; but already before the eighteenth century had begun, music had permanently settled down to a conception of rhythm which I must call body-rhythm. This is the rhythm which the unmusical person enjoys. It is the rhythm not of a talker but of a rider. Only accomplished masters of such rhythm can carry on a conversation through it; and they do not pull at the horse's mouth with every change in the rhythm of their words. Palestrina's *Stabat Mater* begins with some wonderful chords in a rhythm which I set down on the opposite page.

Like all vocal music that is not meant to be realistically or comically dramatic, this is sung considerably slower than the mere declamation of the words; but my notation shows at once that, with that allowance, it is sung to their natural quantities. Palestrina is writing in a homophonic style, so that the voices are all singing together, but he would treat the words exactly in the same way if each voice entered at a different point; and he would build his paragraphs with the same skill that Milton shows in his huge verse paragraphs, by variety in the lengths between the points at which the voices agreed to come to an accented note at the same moment.

Ex.17

How is the rhythm kept together? The chorus-master and every member of the choir counts his pulses, or semibreves (Morley calls them 'strokes'). A time-signature tells us whether two of Morley's strokes go to a breve, and whether two minims go to a stroke. At least ninety per cent of Palestrina's music uses 'imperfect' breves and semibreves—that is to say, notes divided by two. If the time is to be counted by threes, then either or both the breves and the semibreves are 'perfect,' and the time signature is a complete circle. A perpendicular cross-bar to a circle indicates a perfect time whose beats are subdivided by two, and a semicircle indicates duple time, retaining the cross-bar when the composer is reckoning in breves, and being without the cross-bar when he is reckoning in semibreves. Hence, our modern special time-signatures for common and *alla breve* time. Now all this is mere arithmetic, and, so long as the singers and choirmasters kept count of their strokes, there was no reason why the accentuation of the words should be hag-ridden ('ridden' is exactly the right word here, though we need not be dogmatic about the 'hag'). The music was published, or copied, only in parts. Trouble began in the seventeenth century, when, with the rise of instrumental music and operatic performances, it became necessary to range all the parts together on each page for the benefit of the conductor. In order to control the ranging, it was necessary to score the whole page down with parallel lines—hence the term 'score' and the French and German words 'partition' and 'Partitur'. Hence, also, the term 'bar'. At first there was no reason why these partitions should all be of the same size, though they naturally tended to be drawn before an accented note. Handel's rhythm, except in certain interesting particulars of triple time, is entirely familiar to modern ears, but in his autograph scores, if his rhythmic units are short, he will sometimes leave as many as fifteen unbarred. In the score of a full chorus, he is magnificently careless about his ranging, and will perhaps twice in a page conde-scend to draw a necessarily serpentine line from top to bottom of the page to show us who is in step with whom, especially when, as is sometimes necessary, he has to send up a balloon or send down a diving-bell to enclose a bar that has dropped out of a part.

Bach is tidier; but the music of both Bach and Handel moves in rhythmic units which are the same size throughout each compo-sition or self-contained item, and so there has been no reason for dividing, or literally 'scoring', music, whether in print or manu-script, otherwise than by equidistant bars, corresponding to rhythmic group-units. The music, whether it be slow or quick, is riding or dancing. Its rhythm is a body-rhythm, and, while it may adapt itself to undulating ground, it will do so with a swing, and not with jerks. We may not fully understand, but we can enjoy, a vast proportion of classical music in its physically more energetic phases without having cleverer notions of rhythm than the lover of the distant big drum. The general reader need not fear that I must inflict upon him as difficult a description of the elements of musical rhythm as I was compelled to undertake of the elements of tonality.

We can proceed at once to the things which distinguish the great music from the commonplace. Most of the difficulties of Beethoven's rhythm come from the half-knowledge which few who can read musical notation can escape, and which many professional musicians have never outgrown. At the risk of seeming offensive, I will first point out the strange fact that, if a phrase of given length be played at an ambling pace and then be played again eight times as slow, the slow performance will take eight times as long as the amble. This fact is usually overlooked by people who have learnt enough to take in the sense of the phrase and to let the sound take care of itself. If you have enjoyed a symmetrical tune, by the time you have come to the end of it you have an impression of its symmetry not unlike your impression of a symmetrical object in space; and if you can recognize the appearance of such a tune on paper, your imagination will be dangerously apt to take it as read without troubling to include its pace, that is to say, its size, in your idea of it. By the later decades of the nineteenth century, critics and teachers generally told young composers that the slow movement was the main test of power and poetic feeling in a sonata, and that young and merely learned composers were prone therein to show their lack of imagination. The truth is otherwise; in dull works, both learned and inexperienced, the slow move-ment is quite likely to be the best feature, and the scherzos and finales are more usually the worst. When the inexperienced

composer fails in a slow movement, it is not so often because he tries
to be learned and interesting; every critic has warned him against
that. But nobody warns him against the fact that slowness takes
time, which is the chief dimension of music, and so he is apt to
proceed without the slightest notion of the physical size of his
own ideas.

One of the best and most vivid illustrations on this point is
accessible with a pianoforte and a volume of Beethoven's Pianoforte Sonatas, and I have often had occasion to quote it. In the
Adagio of the D minor Sonata, op. 31, no. 2, the main theme is a
16-bar, four-square melody closing into the 17th bar. With an
elementary knowledge of those misleading terms 'binary' and
'ternary' form, the instructed reader recognizes the symmetry of
this object at a glance, usually with the fatal result that, though he
knows that it ought to be played very slowly, he does not imagina-
tively realize that at its proper tempo (M. about 96 to the quaver)
it takes exactly a minute. He thinks of it as he might think of
a letter-weight designed in the shape of the Great Pyramid.
Macaulay knew better, for, though he was no art critic and is
only once recorded to have recognized a tune, he did remark that
absolute size was an important element in architecture, and illustrated this profound aesthetic observation by the Great Pyramid,
for 'what', said he, 'could be more vile than a pyramid thirty feet
high?' The Finale of the D minor Sonata is usually taken too
fast. It is only marked *allegretto*, and a good tempo for it would be
M. 72 to a bar. Thus, 72 bars of this *allegretto* will take exactly as
long as that 16-bar affair in the slow movement. And just see
where this brings you—nearly to the end of the exposition, after
a course of events in which melodies have repeated their later
portions in diminishing fragments, a broad transition has organized
itself on a large scale, and we have had, expanded by emphatic
repetitions, two of the three distinct themes of the second group.
I have found that to some naïve listeners all this sounds actually
shorter than the single main theme of the slow movement. This
will happen if they enjoy a sense of muscular activity more than a
sense of solemn contemplation. But to most people who think
of music in terms of phrase-length the fact that 72 bars of this
Finale are equal to 16 of the slow movement comes as a complete
surprise. Of course, we are not to suppose that the listener is
meant to have a mere clock-sense of time identical for the slow
movement and for the Finale. The art of the composer tells us
'who time ambles withal, who time trots withal, who time gallops
withal, and who he stands still withal'. The opening of this slow
movement would seem to be meant for those who time 'stands
still withal'. But it has an august momentum of its own. The
proper illustration for this is the movement of the earth in its

orbit, a thing of which we are completely unconscious. The earth's speed is many times faster than that of a cannon-ball. How unflattering to our dignity is not the state of universal hustle which science thus reveals! The earth is also a ball, and it takes several minutes to move the length of its own diameter. Our dignity is restored! Now it would be quite possible to mishandle Beethoven's slow movement so that its august momentum was lost. The reader will see at a glance that that immense four-square, 16-bar paragraph is followed by shorter phrases; and, now that he has been duly warned of the danger of seeing musical facts at a glance instead of letting them take their time, he may be allowed to save his own time in this way. But now turn to the beautiful melody that constitutes the second group of the movement—the 8-bar tune in F major that consists of four bars repeating themselves with the difference that the first cadence is medial and is answered by a more final cadence overlapping into the next phrase (bars 31–38). Now, at the join of bar 34/35, the bass moves down to F through the three quavers A, B flat, G. Substitute for this, three quavers C, A, F, leading down to the dominant C, and continue the melody, not with self-repetition, but with a parallel phrase beginning on the dominant. The mischief is already done. We know that we shall have to go round another musical quadrangle of the same size as the opening theme. We have lost our variety of proportion, and all other kinds of external beauty will be powerless to restore it. The form of the whole movement involves a recapitulation of both themes. Beethoven himself, when he came to recapitulate his first theme, adorned the third and fourth sides of its quadrangle with glorious festoons of arpeggio. Even these would still leave the recapitulation almost as disastrous after our 16-bar version of the second theme, and the recapitulation of the expanded second theme would be the worst disaster of all. Beethoven's self-repeated eight bars are as refreshing in their recapitulation as they were on their first appearance.

Now turn to the last six bars of the movement (108–113). Do not put any strain on your conscience by trying to believe that this is not an entirely new theme. Clever people may see some subtle connexion between its curves and the ornamental details of the main theme, but it is a mistake to suppose that the logic of music consists in any such notions. The logic of these six bars is that they reveal the whole rhythmic scale of the movement by bringing us down to human proportions. As I dictate these words, I happen to be pacing up and down the room, and I find that my steps are not too slow for the quavers of this movement. There are six quavers to each of Beethoven's bars, he has hitherto never had a shorter phrase-division than two of these huge bars, and now at last his rhythmic divisions become smaller and smaller, until he is able to give the weight of one of my human footsteps to the unaccented last quaver of the last bar. The logic of this passage is that it reveals the vastness of the whole. Beethoven effects this with a new theme for two reasons. Perhaps his main reason (for he worked by thinking and sketching in music, not by theorizing in words) was that an absolutely new theme would be even more refreshing than Rudyard Kipling's early device of hinting at untold volumes by the phrase, 'But that is another story'; but his practical reason is that he had no previous material that could be broken up into shorter units at all.

Beethoven is, of all composers, the one from whom it is easiest to learn a sense of form and proportion. With Bach, the forms are so regular that a correct description of them is apt to come out like the ground-plan of a Greek temple. Many mechanical imitations of Greek architecture have been made by architects who never discovered the amazing subtlety of the Greek proportions: the 'entasis' and kindred devices by which lines look straight just because they are subtle curves. Mozart and Haydn, whom some people still suppose to be composers for children, are to this extent easier than Bach, that they are dealing with an essentially dramatic art in which the course of events manifestly changes instead of running, in Bach's cumulative way, apparently straight towards its punctual finish. But Haydn and Mozart are composers whose forms are very difficult to describe correctly, and the difficulty is increased by the fact that their language, being that of comedy, is full of irony, while the dramatic events in their music are quiet and not obviously catastrophic. The elements of Beethoven's musical form began fairly early in his career to consist of multiplying the resources of Mozart into those of Haydn. I say multiplying, because, in real works of art, there is no such thing as mere addition. Six and five will make thirty, not eleven, if, indeed, they are not more likely to make 720 ($6 \times 5 \times 4 \times 3 \times 2 \times 1$). Now, when an artist adds enormously to the resources of his predecessors, his results have quite as much the effect of simplification as of complication. Much that was formerly confined is set free for apparently unlimited expansion; but the old material will not stand the new strains and stresses. Mozart's G minor String Quintet shows, to the scandal of some critics, the self-confessed limits of what Mozart's language could express. In art it is always futile to measure one perfection against another; what is right is right then and there; and another work does not become more right by having more elements to handle rightly. In short, if your criticism goes outside the work in hand, all you can say is that what is right for one work will be wrong for another, and it does not matter which work you have happered to consider first. With this caution in mind, we may venture to doubt whether Beethoven ever surpassed the depth and pathos of the slow movement of Mozart's G minor Quintet; he was certainly not ready to suppose that he could, for, before he was too deaf to hear what an orchestra was playing, he exclaimed to a friend during a rehearsal of Mozart's C minor Concerto: 'Ah, such things as this will never occur to the likes of us'; and his appreciation of Mozart and Haydn grew in his later life. But when Mozart comes to write a finale to his G minor Quintet, the best he can do is to write an introduction, tragic in its solemnity, but reserved in its emotional tone, and then frankly to say to his music: 'The rest is too sad for you, my children: run away and play.'

The bright rondo of the G minor Quintet is thus no mere lapse. It is an inadequate finale, but for its inadequacy Mozart nobly apologizes in its solemn introduction. Now Beethoven's new resources removed the language of music from that of comedy of manners, or, rather, raised it to the Shakespearean level, which will always remain hopelessly above the heads of those arbiters of taste who think that tragedy and comedy are less capable of being mixed in art than in life; but the resources that would enable Beethoven to write an adequate finale to Mozart's G minor Quintet are things like his organization of remote changes of key on a rising bass, such as my illustrations from the A major Sonata, op. 2, no. 2, and the *Sonata Appassionata*. And these would have blown Mozart's whole aesthetic system to smithereens. It pleases Milton, in one of the weaker passages in *Paradise Lost*, to imagine the rebel angels discovering gunpowder and doing appreciable damage to Heaven by the artillery of Cromwell's Ironsides. This is not nearly so childish as to speculate what would have happened at Trafalgar if either the French or the English Navy could have brought a Dreadnought to bear upon the situation. Nevertheless, the training of a staff-officer includes a profound study of battles with obsolete resources. These are not the sort of battles he will ever need to plan, but if he does not learn the general art of making his plans according to any and every given scale of dimensions and resources, his brain will degenerate into a mere repository for out-of-date arsenal catalogues. At the same time, he need not expect to find much scope for the use of the Greek phalanx in a modern battle. New resources inevitably crowd out old refinements, though they bring refinements of their own. Thus, Beethoven's rhythm and phrasing are simpler than Haydn's and very much simpler than Mozart's, just because his dramatic and harmonic expression has an enormously larger range.

Consider this again in the light of architecture. If you wish to build a musical cloudscape like Bach's Chromatic Fantasia, or even like the arpeggio preludes in the Forty-Eight, you must build it out of something like nature's materials. Nature builds hers on a scale of many miles in three dimensions, but she builds with air and water-vapour. The painter will not vulgarize his skyscape by making the clouds take the form of a human face, nor will he even think highly of the clever artist who places a harbour-view of the New York skyscrapers beneath a cloudscape which too obviously imitates their outlines. Similarly, Bach will not put Gounod's *Ave Maria* on the top of his First Prelude, quite apart from such a matter of taste as addressing the Virgin with the musical equivalent of 'darling' in the eleventh bar. If he puts melody on the top of an arpeggio prelude at all, it will be as florid as in his E minor Tenth Prelude, where you may notice two things: first, as has already been pointed out, that the bass of this prelude is a very steady descent, so that, if the whole is a cloudscape, it is in a very solid perspective; and secondly, that the melody is so florid that it is more like cirrus clouds than like anything more concrete.

But when Bach is actually working harmonic miracles, as in the Chromatic Fantasia and the 'Et exspecto' of the B minor Mass, he cannot and must not indulge in any themes at all. Still less can he afford to make any rhythmic symmetries. In the last resort, gravitation is as responsible for the behaviour of clouds that are lighter than air as it is for the stability of mountains and the architectural works of man; but even the practical engineer and the practical metallurgist would make little progress in their arts, if they still believed that gravitation was an inherent tendency of bodies to fall unless that tendency was counteracted by the phlogiston which imparts to flame and some air-currents a natural tendency to rise.

There is plenty of what I have called body-rhythm in most of the art of Bach and Handel; but when Bach and Handel are producing recitative, body-rhythm gives way to speech-rhythm; and when Bach is producing cloudscapes, even the speech-rhythm transcends the limits of recitative, and the heavens declare the glory of God with neither speech nor language.

There are one or two cloudscapes in Beethoven, but we shall not find that every passage in which he uses no themes is a cloudscape. On the contrary, his largest acreage of themeless arpeggio is generally architectural, and is apt to consist of tonic and dominant chords followed by a still greater number of final tonic chords. Those of us for whom Nash's Regent Street represented London in its most dignified aspect are apt rather to regret what an American friend of mine has called its 'canyonization' than to do justice to the varied beauties of its new architecture.

An eminent architect has tried to console us by jibing at Nash's extreme economy of thought. We are to be comforted with the reflection that there was nothing in the architecture of the old Regent Street. Now it is very dangerous to speak sarcastically of economy of thought, whether in art or in science. One of the greatest mathematical philosophers has told us somewhere that economy of thought is one of the principal aims and essential characteristics of mathematical research. Certainly, in the fine arts, economy of thought is a vital necessity where the dimensions are large and the largeness is to be employed as an aesthetic fact. In an article in the *Encyclopaedia Britannica*[1] I have illustrated the sonata form by a sketch of the first movement of Beethoven's 'Eroica' Symphony in music type. Here and there the sketch shows, like Beethoven's own early sketches of important works, considerable spaces of blank bars. These I have described as the lungs of the organization. They are as necessary to the planning of good symphonies as parks are to the planning of good towns. The intrusion of themes and counterpoints into these spaces would be as offensive as an irruption of palatial hotels, respectable private houses, bungalows, or slums in Hyde Park. It is the intrusion which is the offence, quite apart from the quality of the intrusive matter. This is not more the case with the passages where Beethoven is arousing expectation than it is when we may say with almost literal truth that all is over except the shouting; as at the end of the C minor Symphony, where the last vestige of a thematic phrase disappears at bar 404 and is followed by 11 bars of tonic and dominant and 29 bars of tonic.

(Let me digress here for a moment to show how the last bar illustrates the philosophic adage that nothing is true which a change of date can make false. Before harmony and counterpoint were evolved, the poet's idea of harmonious music was Milton's 'perfect diapason', which means singing in octaves, and the Greek notion of *symphonia*, which means singing and playing in unison. When absolute finality is in question, this is still quite true. Substitute another complete triad for the final octave of Beethoven's C minor Symphony, and you might almost as well have a downright discord for all the finality you will get after the preceding 28 bars of complete tonic triads.)

The rhythmic analysis of these unadorned architectural features is more difficult than interesting, though there are some clever writers on music who show so little grasp of things as wholes, that they deserve to be dragged through a course of instruction in this matter such as I would never risk inflicting upon a university student. To Bach, it was inconceivable that a piece of music

---

[1] Reprinted in *Musical Articles from the Encyclopaedia Britannica*, by Donald Francis Tovey. Oxford University Press.

should end otherwise than with the last note of a melodically significant phrase, except in the case of such cloudscapes as his arpeggio preludes, and even these retain their individual style down to the last note, whether they end in a regular rhythmic period or die away over a tonic pedal. Handel will often interrupt his last cadence with a pause, followed by a grand *Amen* to be played extremely slowly and with full force. In the storm and stress of experimental modern music, many listeners and a considerable number of our younger composers find a blessed relief in the all-pervading punctuality of Bach. But we shall have seen only the outward symptoms of this quality if we cannot also see its essentials in the punctuality of Beethoven's final formulas. By all means let us cry 'Back to Bach' if we mean to rise to Bach; but the slogan is often no better than an inability to recognize poetry in any form other than Miltonic blank verse, and from this the next step is to deplore the absence of rhyme and win our way to the Promised Land of the heroic couplet.

The punctuality of Beethoven's art is, then, a punctuality of movement that cannot be detected by an analysis of themes and other externals of his art-forms. Beethoven's punctuality can be sadly impaired in the performances of persons who have no sense of form. There is, for instance, a famous gramophone record of his Violin Concerto, as played by one of the most celebrated living violinists, which displays the solo violin to great advantage and is from phrase to phrase unimpeachably noble in its rendering, but intolerably slow and utterly without regard for the doubtless trivial detail that the orchestra often accompanies the florid solo part by a main theme. Hardly more vulgar is the habit of hurrying Beethoven's formal finalities after the thematic interest has expired. You will sometimes find, as in the C minor Symphony, that Beethoven will give a direction, *stringendo*, or *accelerando*, which will lead to *presto*, but you will never find the faintest hint that the 'presto', once attained, is to be further accelerated. The presto at the end of the C minor Symphony is indicated 82 bars before the end. The presto at the end of the Overture to *Leonore*, No. 3, is emotionally far more intense, inasmuch as that overture is throughout a dramatic process in itself, whereas the whole Finale of the C minor Symphony is from its outset a final triumph; but the *Leonore* final presto is 125 bars long, starts at its full speed at once, and merely loses force if the conductor accelerates any part of it.

Of course, much depends on the actual pace, but this itself depends also on acoustic and technical conditions. With different orchestras and different concert-rooms, the ideal pace will differ: the fastest advisable pace will be that in which it is still possible to hear distinctly. Weingartner has remarked that he takes the

Finale of Beethoven's Seventh Symphony slower than most conductors, and that he usually gets either praised or blamed for his
tremendous pace. Beethoven's own metronome tempi are a very
bad guide, being, like most composers' tempi, far too fast. The
only exception is the Ninth Symphony, where he had an opportunity of testing the matter properly. He then reduced his tempi
by about two-thirds—e.g. the first movement, marked in the
autograph at $\quarternote$=120 was reduced to $\quarternote$=88! A hundred years
later, we find Reger carefully metronomizing all his works, but
adding as a footnote that these marks are to be taken only as the
extreme permissible limit of speed; and Reger himself, in playing
or controlling a performance of his works, never approached
within two-thirds of his own printed marks. Tempo rubato is
an important matter about which our critics are at present going
through a very pedantic phase. A good tempo rubato is a natural
freedom, such as that of horse and rider where the rider has a
good seat and the ground is neither hard nor dead-level. My
objection to a certain record of Beethoven's Violin Concerto is
not even that the violinist displays a bad rubato, but that for
whole minutes at a time he displays no tempo at all, and that it
is only in the orchestral tuttis that the music has any coherence.
The solo part is all very emotional: I will not say sentimental,
because this might be taken to imply false or ignoble sentiments
and vicious over-indulgences in the portamento and vibrato.
From these vices the sentiment is nobly free, but, unfortunately,
it is to this extent false, that its musical causes (the only ones
that concern the listener) have disappeared beyond the reach of
psycho-analysis. A good rubato is not only entirely consistent with
the momentum of what I call body-rhythm in music, but is a
necessary consequence of it. One good rule-of-thumb test for it,
as for all freedom, is this—that true freedom emphasizes distinctions, or, if you will, exaggerates them, whereas false freedom
obliterates them. Lest we fall into vulgar political confusions
about the meaning of 'distinctions', let us be perfectly clear that
to emphasize true distinctions also means to obliterate false ones.
Few, if any, of our musical theorists seem to have appreciated
the enormous momentum of the rhythms of sonata-music in
Haydn, Mozart, and Beethoven. Brahms devoted one-half of his
musical life to lyric music and the other half (more energetic,
though quantitatively less prolific) to the recovery of the lost
momentum of classical music. Wagner's mature music-drama has
a momentum of its own, needing his whole dramas in which to
express itself, and hardly able to appear in concert extracts at
all. On Wagner's huge scale, a phenomenon has arisen which
has become a commonplace in other music—viz. the gradual
change of one tempo to another, apart from such incidents as the

accelerando leading to the final presto of Beethoven's Fifth Symphony. Now, when one tempo can thus change imperceptibly to a totally different one, the result, whatever its own merits, must be incompatible with the classical momentum. You cannot change the pace of your horse or check your own athletic movements, either suddenly or gradually, without knowing what you are doing. But it is not uncommon in post-classical music, both conservative and revolutionary, for the composer to start like an athlete controlling his own muscles or his own mount, and to continue like a passenger by rail or motor. In such a case, as far as energy is concerned, the faster he travels the sooner he will go to sleep.

When a composer states a slow melody in its own proper tempo, and afterwards, during the course of a quick movement, allows this melody to float, in something like its original dimensions, over the quicker material, he must be a great master of musical momentum if any real effect of contrast is to arise at all. In Berlioz's *Romeo and Juliet*, the music that describes the Capulets' feast begins with one of Berlioz's slow melodies descriptive of the love which springs up between Romeo and Juliet. Then there is a lively movement describing the festivities. At the climax of this, Berlioz proudly calls attention to the *réunion des deux thèmes*, and the love-theme written in semibreves floats in its original tempo over the festive theme. The composition has other merits, but as far as movement is concerned, this combination merely reveals what has already been open to suspicion, that the festive theme, for all its leg-shakings and twitchings, never had any power of movement at all. In *Tannhäuser*, Wagner's mastery of music is not as advanced as his mastery of drama, but he already shows more momentum than Berlioz when the slow Pilgrims' Chorus of the Introduction first returns over the witches'-cauldron dying reverberations of the *Venusberg*. For Wagner does not at once put the Pilgrims' Chorus into its original triple time, but squares up its rhythm to fit that of the allegro. Only when the chorus swells out to full power does the original slow triple time dominate everything, while the violins pour out their cascades of bell-ringers' scales at full speed. Wagner understands what he is doing, and though the result is obvious and far below his mature art, it is exciting enough; but you must turn to the end of *Götterdämmerung* to see how it is possible to display the grandeur of the burning of *Valhalla* while keeping up and enhancing the momentum of the swift climax of human and sub-human tragedy below. (I say advisedly sub-human, because Bernard Shaw is clearly right in saying that Wagner's human beings are intentionally greater than his gods and half-human actors.) You will find three cases of musical momentum equally powerful and equally manifest here—the slow 3/2 time of *Valhalla*; the broad common-time of the so-called *Erlösung* motive, pronouncing to the world a final message of redemption by love; and, throughout the whole climax, all the delightful energy of the 6/8 time at the beginning of *Das Rheingold* as the Rhine-maidens swim upon the flood holding in triumph their recovered gold. Beethoven had no opportunities for experimenting with such combinations of tempo, but, if you look at the Overture to *Leonore*, No. 3, and see what becomes of Florestan's air when, after having stated it near the beginning of the slow Introduction, he adapts it to the purposes of his second group in the allegro without slackening his pace, you will soon see that his semibreves not only maintain his allegro, but that they lead to modulations of which the action is as rapid as anything the allegro can do; and you will not find it difficult to imagine the theme being cast in 3-bar rhythm so as to maintain its original adagio aspect; and, if you can imagine this, you will see at once that the allegro would from that moment have sagged beyond hope of recovery. Some years ago an eminent critic praised Rossini at the expense of Mozart because of Rossini's extraordinary sense of pace. There is a great deal of patter-singing in Rossini's *Barbiere*, and most of it is very fast indeed, but it is not as fast as the patter-singing that Mozart gives to the most decrepit character in his *Figaro*. Mozart's less decrepit characters have more to say and more to do. Patter-singing he leaves to old lawyers who have to read documents and produce precedents in court.

Now let us take a lesson from Beethoven in the art of changing a tempo. The Fourth Symphony, coming between the 'Eroica' and the C minor, is one of those masterpieces which many people insist on despising for being satisfied with its own size. Only a master who could produce the 'Eroica' Symphony could have produced this smaller work at all, and, as with the Eighth Symphony, which stands in a similar position between the Seventh and the Ninth, Beethoven felt even more strongly the sense that his powers were extending than when he was producing larger works. As a study in movement, the Fourth Symphony reveals things that we simply have not leisure to notice in larger works. I here refer to the passage in which the Allegro has comfortably settled down to its pace. I am speaking of the momentum, not of the tempo, which is asserted at the outset. The momentum would soon merely send us to sleep if nothing happened from time to time to change it. That is the trouble with so much post-classical music. Few composers seem to realize that, when all your phrases are the same length and all your changes of colour and pattern at equal distances, you may cry 'Faster, faster,' like the *Looking-Glass* Red Queen when she ran poor Alice to breathlessness and then dumped her at the foot of the same tree that had overshadowed them all the time.

Now let us see how Beethoven asserts his 'allegro vivace'. The introduction has been so slow that the young Weber, who was outspoken and honest and died before he had time to understand Beethoven, laughed at it as a display of the knack of spreading the fewest possible notes over a quarter of an hour. So, at all events, he did see something extraordinary in the size of it, which is just what nowadays escapes the intelligence of musicians who can take things in at a glance. This introduction is very quiet, very dark, and tragically mysterious. Tragedies do not often begin in this way. Such darkness arouses expectations, the fulfilment of which may be disappointing. But the contradiction of them may be very refreshing. Weber exaggerates when he talks of a quarter of an hour. Beethoven has kept us in darkness for not much over two minutes; then, with very little warning, the whole orchestra bursts out with two mighty crashes, still in the slow tempo and on the home dominant, now established as that of a major key after the many mysterious and remote modulations of the introduction; and now, here, the crashes are followed up with a drastically clear assertion of the full speed of the allegro vivace. We are, so to speak, hustled into the saddle, and our horse prances off at once. Then comes a playful theme, which consists of four bars closing into four answering bars, the last two of which are unexpectedly prolonged and are followed by two fortissimo bars on the lines of the first crash into the allegro. Then the theme is repeated as a tutti, and its close expanded by further bars. After this, nothing in Rossini could give us so glorious a sense of running comfortably at full speed.

It would be an exaggeration to say that the logic of music lay wholly, or even mainly, in these matters of phrase-length, but it is quite certain that it lies in nothing less than the whole [musical] structure, and the chapters on tonality have already shown that, if a return to the home tonic is not associated with thematic or other formal evidence of its intention, it may be entirely unrecognizable except as a piece of professional information, probably aesthetically misleading to persons who happen to have a sense of absolute pitch. But it is quite certain that there is more logic inherent in the masterly handling of phrase-rhythms than in any ingenuities by which one theme can be derived from another.

I cannot pursue this branch of the subject any farther. The reader will probably be able to follow it up for himself. By way of giving him the first step towards independence, I would call his attention to the varying size of the phrases in the finale of the D minor Sonata, op. 31, no. 2, just at the point where my selected minute was up—viz. from bars 67/72 and onwards. There are two useful terms for processes in the sonata style which are common and obviously stimulative of the sense of movement. You may talk of 'tapering' rhythm when the composer, having stated, say, an 8-bar melody, repeats the last four bars of that, and then the last two bars, then the last bar and the last notes, and this kind of tapering is not much more difficult to recognize when its elements are new instead of being repetitions. Similarly, 'expanding' rhythm will begin with short items and continue by doubling, or otherwise increasing, the phrase-lengths. In the exposition of the first movement of the Fourth Symphony, the sense of comfortable settled pace goes with 8-bar phrases, and the tendency is to break these up into shorter elements, until, in one very characteristic passage, we have sequences of which the steps are a bar-and-a-half, with a resulting cross-accent that is very exciting. After the double-bar and repeat (it is a crime to omit the repeat in this movement), there comes the development, and, as we shall see in dealing with Beethoven's art-forms, the word 'development' is applied to a part of a movement that corresponds more or less with the principal imbroglio of a novel or play. Ingenious contrapuntal combinations may be of use in a development, but they cannot of themselves produce more than an argumentative effect. To develop a theme dramatically, we again need the power to change the size of its phrases and to combine it with other themes rather by building new tunes in partnership with them than by contrapuntal combination. In both the first movement and in the innocent-seeming Finale of Beethoven's Fourth Symphony, the developments are conspicuous examples of the value of wide open spaces. We might recommend the first movement of the Fourth Symphony as a breathing exercise to listeners, who may try and hold their breath according to the phrase-lengths. But perhaps the breathing exercise will come of itself in a more beneficial form if we listen to the music without thinking of anything else.

PHRASING AND ACCENT

THOUGH Beethoven's phrasing is not as intricate as Mozart's, it is still too difficult to be dealt with adequately in the present volume; but the reader need not let this interfere with his enjoyment of Beethoven, nor need he suppose that Beethoven's phrasing is beyond his comprehension. It is merely one of those things of which the proverbially intelligent child says: 'Thanks, I can understand perfectly if only you won't explain.' But in order to attain that child's innocent intelligence, we must, as usual, remove some debris of professional obstructions. Profane parodists have alleged the existence of an old-fashioned type of sermon in which the preacher stresses each word of the text in turn, drawing a different moral from the effect of each stress. In this way, the length of the sermon can be secured without more than mechanical labour in the composition. And it is conceivable that on this plan sermons may have been produced with a quality of thought considerably less stupid than the plan. Certainly, it is hardly possible to find a pregnant sentence which will not bear considering in varying lights according as you stress this word or that. And this is not less true of musical sentences. Nor are great composers more ready than other great writers to commit themselves or their interpreters to one exclusive way of stressing their sentences. The instructive editors of classical music are for the most part terrible dogmatists in this matter, and against some of their dogmas every first-rate interpreter, with Joachim at the head, is in revolt.

The chief means of indicating phrasing by musical notation is by slurs drawn over the notes. Attempts have been made to distinguish the use of these slurs as phrase-marks from their use as articulations into 'legato' and 'staccato' depending on the instruments for which the composer is writing. By my share in the edition of Beethoven's Pianoforte Sonatas published by the Associated Board of the Royal Schools of Music, I am responsible for such attempts, but in my preface to that edition I have done my best to point out that no consistent results are to be expected from them, and that, where Beethoven has not chosen to make up his mind, he does not invite us to make it up for him. Ambiguities are of different kinds. There is the stupid ambiguity of the slovenly writer; there is the malicious diplomatic ambiguity of the oracle and the casuist; and, lastly, there is the ambiguity, or many-sided significance, of all great writing, which it is folly to reduce to a single meaning, since all its meanings are true and consistent with each other.

So much, then, will suffice for the intricacies of phrasing; but the reader will need more definite information about Beethoven's accentuation; or, at all events, he will need the definite correction of certain prevalent misunderstandings about it.

We have already discussed sixteenth-century rhythm, and so far we have not encountered any reason to suppose that the powerful body-rhythm and immense momentum of Beethoven's music could have anything to do with the speech-rhythms of Palestrina. Yet it is just where Beethoven's rhythms are most dance-like that we encounter ambiguities and positive changes of stress that will not cease to puzzle us, as they puzzle many editors, until we have recovered some of the elastic notions of rhythm that Palestrina can teach us. It is a pity that the ambiguities do not more often puzzle the editors. Usually, the editors are quite cock-sure about them and insist upon destroying them. The most important, and the most vivid, examples of the point in question are in Beethoven's scherzos. Why does Beethoven write all his scherzos in the shortest possible bars? The result is often very inconvenient, not only to the analytic student, but to the actual performers and conductors, who wish to know where the accent should fall in the more flowing phrases. It is impossible to construe the marvellous third movement of the C minor Symphony unless you realize that it is in the second full bar that the first rhythmic accent occurs. It will be convenient to call notes before the first accent of a phrase by the same name which we give to syllables before the first accent in a line of poetry—viz. *anacrusis*. The first four notes of the Scherzo of the C minor Symphony are, then, an anacrusis. Nobody can tell us whether the first bar of the first movement is an anacrusis. Weingartner makes out that sometimes it is and sometimes it is not, and he shows that there is a certain symmetry in the way in which the two cases alternate. The Scherzo of the Seventh Symphony puzzles us in the same way. If you march to its bars, the loudness of the first bar will certainly start you off at once, but you will have reason to suspect that you are out of step before you reach the double-bar; and later on you will find that, if you were in step with the main theme at first, you will be out of step when it enters in the oboe in B flat at bar 69. But if you then correct your step, you will find that, after all, bar 90 will violently jerk you back again. Take, again, the exquisite little Allegretto of the C sharp minor ('Moonlight') Sonata. You can read the whole movement either as having an anacrusis of one crotchet, or as having an anacrusis of a crotchet and a bar. If you take the second view, the sforzandos in the trio will be a cross-accent; and why not? Similarly, in the Scherzo of the A flat Sonata, op. 110, Beethoven writes in 2/4 bars, which deprives us of all means of knowing whether the rhythm is that of a gavotte with the first two notes as an anacrusis, or whether the accent is on the first note. Whichever way you take it, you will find an odd bar somewhere in the trio. On the whole, the gavotte view makes the best sense, for, though Beethoven has put the word *coda* on the first of the minim chords in the last line of the movement instead of a bar earlier, it is difficult to make sense of those chords unless you think of them as lying across the accent. In the scherzo of the E flat 'Fantasia' Sonata, op. 27, no. 1, it is really necessary to know that the whole first bar is an anacrusis, and there Beethoven has helped us by putting his double-bar before the second bar, at the cost of having to write it again as a *prima volta* bar when he marks the repeat. In the scherzo of the A flat Sonata, op. 26, doubts have been raised about the bass of the 10th bar of its second part, which most commentators wish to carry on in thirds with the treble, in flat contradiction to the very legible autograph. These doubts can never arise as soon as we understand that the complete first full bar of the trio is an anacrusis. The whole rhythmic question is very like the optical trick which is played upon us by a pattern of square tiles of alternating colour set cornerwise. When you fix your eye on any point in this pattern, if what you see appears as a perspective of one cube on the top of two cubes, it will soon change into two cubes on the top of one.

But why does Beethoven tolerate all these ambiguities, when, by taking longer bars, he could place the position of the accents beyond doubt? The obvious answer is that he enjoys the doubt. He would be thoroughly in sympathy with the militiamen immortalized in the pages of *Punch* by the pencil of John Leech or Charles Keene: 'Jim, ye bain't in step.' 'Bain't I? Well, then, change yourn.' He is a tiresome companion for a walk, who always insists in your keeping step with him, and who will interrupt his own as well as your talk with '*Left*, right, *left*, right'. The plain fact is that, in these dance movements, Beethoven wishes for a habit of equally hard accent for all the shortest rhythmic units; not, of course, anything grotesque or incompatible with smoother phrasing, but a rhythm definitely too energetic in its steps to make us ready to think one beat more important than another. In fact, the bar-strokes, which are a typographical nuisance so destructive to our perception of the freedom of sixteenth-century rhythm, have become useful to Beethoven in expressing the freedom of his scherzo rhythms. In the Scherzo of the Ninth Symphony, he has a famous passage in 3-bar rhythm which he marks *Ritmo di tre battute*, and he also carefully marks the point, otherwise imperceptible, where the rhythm returns to *Ritmo di quattro battute*. The reason why he has given us no such help in earlier works is not, as has often been supposed, because the Ninth Symphony shows a great increase in rhythmic elaboration which makes positive directions necessary, but, on the contrary, because in the earlier works the rhythmic irregularities were capricious, whereas in the Ninth Symphony they have simplified themselves into bigger processes. It would still be a complete mistake to save Beethoven the trouble of his directions for *Ritmo di tre battute* by rewriting the scherzo in 12/4 or 12/8 and changing to 9/8 when necessary. This would merely turn it into something as smooth as the *Saltarello* of Mendelssohn's Italian Symphony, whereas, if you want to ride such a thoroughbred as the Scherzo of the Ninth Symphony, you must be constantly ready to rise in your stirrups at every one of Beethoven's short bars.

In Beethoven's works, you will more often encounter the opposite kind of evidence that the bar is still a typographical device rather than a constant rhythmic unit. When Beethoven writes a movement in moderate or slow common-time, you will be sure to find passages which, on a repetition either immediately or at a distance, come half a bar out. This does not mean any shifting of accent at all. On the contrary, Mozart prefers common-time to 2/4 time because he does not wish for hard accents. In the exquisite and deliberately popular (*volkstümlich*) duet *Bei Männern welche Liebe fühlen* in *Die Zauberflöte*, the theme is a gently swinging 6/8, and the autograph shows that Mozart had reached the end of it before he found that one of his odd half-bars was displacing the last cadence in a way that, with this amount of lilt, was too awkward to pass. Accordingly, he altered the position of the bars from the outset. He preferred this to taking 3/8 bars as his unit, because he did not want his gentle lyric to set up too energetic a body-rhythm. Throughout the nineteenth century our rhythmic notions were so bar-ridden that even as devoted a Mozart-lover as Otto Jahn had the impertinence to say that Mozart's rhythmic sense was weak in such matters. On the contrary, it was as strong and delicate as the proverbial steam-hammer that can crack a nut, and it is we, with our bell-metro-nomes, who in these rhythmic matters support our feeble knees and spines with crutches.

The Beethoven-lover's best course in these, as in all musical matters, is to clear his mind of all professional cant and trust Beethoven. If he takes a fall now and then, it will do him no harm. The spirit of Beethoven's own advice would probably be in harmony with that of the steward of the Clyde steamer, who, when the passenger was querulous about the saloon-stairs, cheerfully said: 'Let go yer hands and yer feet, and ye'll come down by yersel'.'

BEETHOVEN'S ART-FORMS

WE are now in a position to discuss what is commonly called form in Beethoven without falling into the common errors of a bird's-eye view of music. Except for the fact that the technical terms are peculiar to music, it is ridiculously easy to describe either the outlines or the rules of any musical form: the outlines, when the form is analogous to a shape; the rules, when, like fugue, the form is analogous to a texture such as blank verse. Controversies, more or less acrimonious, may arise over questions of terminology. The reader may neglect these. They are not cases where doctors differ, but cases where the terminology is irrelevant. I shall use a terminology of my own, which will explain itself in the course of discussion, and I shall give the reader timely warning of current misuses.

The vast majority of Beethoven's work is, as we have already seen, related to the sonata forms. With these forms two great principles must be clearly understood. The first principle is that the sonata style is inveterately dramatic. This has been already abundantly illustrated in the previous chapters, and familiarity cannot fail to impress it more and more deeply on the listener. The second principle is more difficult to grasp and to describe; and failure to grasp it is the origin of many confusions in current ideas of sonata-style. The point is this: that sonata form and style arise just at the breaking-point between lyric melody and dramatic music. From this results a tangle of disastrous confusion because of the external resemblance between the features of genuine sonata-style and those of melodic forms that have not broken away into dramatic musical action. The term 'second subject' displays and stimulates the worst of all confusions on this question. Clever writers tell us that Bach and his fellow polyphonists worked with one principal subject, while the sonata-writers work with two. Writers who use such terminology show little agreement among themselves over what they mean by the word 'subject'; but they probably agree with the normally intelligent reader in supposing that it means much the same as 'theme'. English writers neglect to tell the reader anything about foreign terminology, and, beyond remarking that the German terms *Hauptsatz*, *Seitensatz*, and *Schlussgruppe* are much more noncommittal than the English terms, I shall be equally neglectful. Themes are extremely important in the sonata forms, but the reader had better make up his mind at once that all attempts to lay down rules for their number and position are mistaken. The terms I shall use are as follows: Exposition, Development,

Recapitulation, Coda, First Group, Second Group, Episode, First-movement Form, Rondo, Counterstatement, Transition. For fugues and variations I shall have another set of terms; but in all cases the reader will find that an ordinary English dictionary is a safe guide to the meaning of my terms.

The exposition of any movement is that part of it which exposes the principal material. In first-movement form, it will contain a first group and a second group. These groups are what the old terminology so misleadingly calls first and second subjects. The reason why these old terms are misleading is that they have never been properly distinguished from themes, and that there are no rules for the number of themes in either group. The subject of a fugue is its theme. I am compelled to avoid the use of the word 'subject' in talking of sonata form at all, because nobody seems to be sure, or, rather, a great many people seem to be far too sure, that it means a whole group, and this doctrine drives them to painful ingenuities in deriving all sorts of different themes from one another, when the composer has no such derivations in his mind. Such casuistry becomes all the worse from the fact that, as composers become more experienced, their style is apt to grow more allusive and witty, so that the fascinating tissue of connecting-links develops between all parts of their work. Then come whole schools of composition, like those of Vincent d'Indy and Stanford, which inculcate that the main stresses of musical architecture can actually be undertaken by such connective tissue; and such teachings may even draw some support from the naïve advice of the veteran Haydn, when he said that young composers should not waste a large number of ideas on one movement, but should see how much they can make of one idea: advice according to which Haydn himself ought to have written no early works at all. The question-begging word in such advice is the word 'idea'. The experienced composer can make one theme give rise to any number of delightfully different ideas; but these are not derived from one another by machinery, and their difference is aesthetically more important than their identity. A young composer will be better advised to put into his early works as many different themes as Haydn, Mozart, and Beethoven put into theirs, and to wait for experience to give him the power to get genuinely different ideas out of one theme. Many errors in musical criticism arise from unconscious dogmatic assumptions about what constitutes a musical idea. The word 'idea' can be safely used in its ordinary English sense, qualified only by the epithet 'musical'. An eminent critic once accused Beethoven of lack of concentration in the slow movement of the Ninth Symphony, because Beethoven abandoned his idea as soon as he had stated it, the ground for this charge being that the movement contains two themes, not only in widely different keys, but at different paces and with different time-signatures. These two themes are, no doubt, ideas; and, as it is unusual, though not unprecedented, in classical music, to bring together ideas in such different tempi, the critic inferred that Beethoven had lost his grip of his subject, or his main idea. But the critic happened to have missed a very much bigger main idea, which covers the whole movement, and this idea is precisely what no naïve listener who can be thrilled by a change of harmony could possibly miss, even if he has not stimulated his power of recognizing such things at the cost of burdening his memory with my tables of key-relations. At the point in question, where Beethoven has 'abandoned his idea as soon as he has stated it', the last dying fall of his repeated strain leads to the bright chord of the major mediant, which turns out to be the tonic of the new theme in a new key and time. The change of time is a great surprise; the four-square self-repeated symmetry of the new theme is, like the second theme of the slow movement of opus 31, no. 2, in well-proportioned contrast to the longer phrases and expansive reverberations of the main theme. Without loss of more time than that of two echoing bars with a dark modulation back to the home tonic, the main theme returns in a variation. At this point, let me explain that I shall always use the word 'variation' in its special musical sense of an uninterrupted and complete statement of a whole theme in varied guise. The variation inevitably reaches the same bright D major (III) chord. This time the chord proves to be a dominant, and the second theme is given, with varied scoring, in G major (VI). When its last echo passes into a dark modulation, that modulation will necessarily lead, not to the home tonic, but to its subdominant, E flat, and the main theme, resumed in that key, shows that it does not wish to stay there, but wanders meditatively through a remoter and darker region which (finding itself to be ♭II) resolves itself into the home tonic, and so swings into a glorious new variation of the whole main theme; and now what is to happen to the bright modulation at the end? The dying fall has twice served its dramatic purpose of leading to a new theme in remote keys. Its final task is to lead to the subdominant as a typical position in which the coda, or peroration, of the whole poem should begin. This it effects in the grandest style, and, as I have said before, the naïve listener, if he has an uncorrupted harmonic sense, cannot possibly miss either the structural or the emotional effects of those three different turns to the close of the main theme. It is indeed fatally possible to miss these points if one's notions of harmony have suffered from the diet of stale scraps and crumbs served up in harmony-books. There are practical difficulties in teaching musical or any other grammar except in short sentences and paradigms of declensions and verbs, which, no doubt for logical reasons, include sesquipedalian pluperfects that have never been found in any decent Greek prose; but you can neither make nor understand a good literary style on the basis of sentences constructed mainly for the purpose of a complete catalogue of grammatical forms. Perhaps that is not only one reason why Beethoven is supposed to have contributed so little to the development of harmony, but also a possible reason why nowadays, when we are all so anxious to develop a new harmony, there is so little sense of movement and composition in the average output of modern music. This was not so in Beethoven's time. It is quite probable that, of the music that is talked about nowadays, as large a proportion may survive a hundred years hence as has survived of the output of the eighteenth and early nineteenth centuries; but, if you have the patience to dip into the stuff contemporary with Beethoven which has not survived, you will find that, though its sense of movement amounts to no more than a comfortable amble, it can maintain that pace like a serviceable and good-tempered moke. You may even find that such music may give refined pleasure, if good playing will keep a carrot steadily projected in front of the moke's nose. In fact, there is always a danger that this refined pleasure may come into fashion at the biddance of people who cannot endure anything so big as Beethoven, and there are signs of this revolution in some of the neo-classicists of the present day, who are not rediscovering Mozart and early Beethoven, but are taking refuge in much less vital things. Still, even this will do them more good than harm, if the jerry-building of stiff sonata-forms can accidentally teach them some of the lost art of composition.

The slow movement of Beethoven's Ninth Symphony is a good initiation into Beethoven's art-forms, for precisely the reason that it is unique, and so forces us to attend to its individual details instead of turning them into actuarial statistics by classification. With all works of art, the actuarial view is even more misleading than the bird's-eye view of music. The office that insures your life has no means of knowing whether you will live up to the expectation of the doctor, or whether you will be run over by a motor-bus five minutes after you have taken out your policy. You had better not be any wiser about the course of events in Beethoven's most conventional sonata until you have listened to it moment by moment from beginning to end. If it falls in with conventional form, that is because the form has become conventional from having very often been the most beautiful way of dealing with certain kinds of material. At first sight, the rules of sonata form must seem to be highly conventional, and it is difficult to imagine them as not existing *a priori*. I very much doubt whether they are anything like as conventional as the rules of architectural forms, nor do I believe that architecture is to be understood, any more than music, by treating the rules as moulds outside the work, instead of as principles of growth from within. This question is quite independent of practical composition; if an artist cannot escape knowing hundreds of works that are similar in form, he cannot escape knowing beforehand that his own compositions will be apt to take such forms. What is important is that we should never lose sight of the vitality of a genuine work of art by imagining either that when a composer produces an unusual form he 'breaks the mould', or that when he produces a usual one he is restricting himself by convention.

When an art-form is at once manifestly vital and subject to apparently elaborate conventions, this may be taken as a sign that its materials exist on a border-line between two opposing conditions. I have already suggested that most of the phenomena of sonata form and all the difficulties in explaining it come from the fact that it represents music at the breaking-point between lyric unity and dramatic variety. I shall use the term 'melodic' for forms that are on so small a scale that we apprehend them as single melodies. There is an abominably vague term, 'Lied-form', used by many writers with a manner of precision which impresses me all the more since I have never been able to find out what the term means. The forms which are small enough to be apprehended as melodic comprise many things that it would be vexatious to classify. What can be more futile, for example, than to invent a technical term for the form of the tune '*Wachet auf*' ('Sleepers, wake, a voice is calling')? But when the late J. B. Dykes took the salient features of that tune and carved them into his nice little four-square hymn-tune to the words, 'Holy, holy, holy, Lord God Almighty', he achieved a typical specimen of what is called binary form, inasmuch as the first half of his tune ends on the dominant, while the second half ends on the tonic.

The terms 'binary' and 'ternary' correspond to certain accidents of form both on melodic and on a larger scale; and this is most unfortunate, because the features which seem to justify their existence happen to mask the vital points of difference between two classes of melody and form. *God Save the King* is what is commonly called a ternary tune, inasmuch as its first six bars end on the tonic. At first sight this reason seems to be insufficient, but it is a fact that such tunes have a tendency, not shown by *God Save the King*, to fall definitely into three parts, the third part being a more or less complete repetition of the first; actually, this matter of falling into two or three parts is not vital. The listener will feel an instinctive distrust of all such map-like divisions if he has acquired the genuine musical habit of listening to music as a process in time. He will distinguish binary forms from ternary, neither by wisdom after the event, nor by an impossibly prophetic sense that he is going to hear two portions or three, but by something self-evident at the moment when the music chooses between the so-called binary and ternary courses: and this self-evident thing is that, in what is commonly called binary, the first articulate member of the form is incomplete, as shown by its not ending on the tonic; whereas, in the so-called ternary form, the first member is complete. And this explains why so many melodies of this second class do fall into three parts.

If the first member is complete, the sequel has to make its own effort to go farther afield, and is therefore likely to become a middle section, from which the natural conclusion is something like a *da capo* of the first section. The convenient symbol for such a form is A B A. If B is as complete as A, then the result is too stiff to pretend to unity. There is no reason why the phrase should not be put together in this specially stiff way; but, in the wonderful Rondo of Beethoven's E minor Sonata, op. 90, you may, if you like, consider that the main theme consists of AA BB AA. Even here, the term 'ternary' misses the point. In the first place, the A is not a repeated strain of four bars, but a self-repeating 8-bar strain. Though the cadence into bar 4 is tonic, it is melodically obviously not final, as is its answer in bar 8. In the second place, B is twice as slow, or, as we had better call it, twice as large, as A, inasmuch as it consists of 8 bars that are not self-repeating; but this whole 8-bar strain is repeated. The proper way to regard the whole 32-bar section is not to classify it at all, but to treat it as unique.

Another unique rondo-opening is that of the D major Sonata, op. 28, commonly called 'Pastorale'. It is absurd to invent technical terms for so gloriously naïve a collocation of ideas. It is not even worth while considering whether the ideas are repeated or self-repeating. If you wish to feel technically wise about this opening, you will have grasped the main point when you have noticed that bars 9–16 move twice as fast as bars 1–8.

Now take the most genuinely ternary melodies conceivable—melodies of A B A form in which A is completely reproduced at the end and B contributes to the unity of the whole by refraining from being complete in itself. The acid test of melodic forms comes when we repeat their members. It is possible to repeat the first six bars of *God Save the King*, though I am not aware that words have ever been designed for the procedure, or that it has ever been customary; but Beethoven, when he wrote a set of variations on it, an early and unsatisfactory *opusculum*, did repeat both the first six bars and the remaining eight, in the theme and in the variations. The tune obviously does not divide into three parts; but it is quite clear that the theme of the variations in the 'Kreutzer' Sonata divides into three, and there are natural reasons why its members should be repeated, especially in its first announcement, where the pianoforte has the first statement and the violin the second. Now try the experiment of repeating it on the plan AA BB AA. Even if, on its first statement, you alter the last bar of B so as to counteract its irresistible urge to return to A, the total effect of marking your threefold division by repeats is so absurd that you will need no further evidence that the only possible division for such a melody is into A and BA. This is the last time I shall use the words 'binary' and 'ternary'. They are manifestly quite unilluminating, when they are not actually misleading. Nobody has as yet invented terms that will express the real difference between these two main types of form—that in which the first member is incomplete, and that in which it is complete. One thing is evident from the outset: that a much higher unity in diversity—that is to say, a much higher organization—will arise from the type with an incomplete first member, so-called binary, than from the type with a complete first member. The former type gives rise on a large scale to the great first-movement forms of the sonata. The A B A type gives rise to lyric forms and rondo forms. It is worth while distinguishing between a properly continuous A B A with an incomplete B and the collocation which outwardly resembles it, where two equally complete objects are put together as minuet, trio, and da capo. Such distinctions do concern the listener, because, while he ought not to set up an affectation of superiority to sectional features in music, he ought to appreciate all evidences of a higher unity behind the obvious sections.

Melodic forms can expand to considerable length without transcending the melodic range. The wonderful Allemande of Bach's D major Partita takes quite six minutes if played with both its repeats, and the person who can deny that it has at least three distinct themes will deny anything. Both Haydn and Beethoven have written large and dramatic movements that are shorter and have fewer themes. This does not mean that Bach's largest suite-movements show any tendency towards the essentials of sonata style, and still less does it show anything archaic in Haydn's economy of themes. At the same time, it is very doubtful whether many of Haydn's, or even of Beethoven's, contemporaries fully realized the radical change that had come over the whole art of music coincidently with Gluck's reform of opera. Haydn's warmest admirer, Boccherini, and many other composers, continued to produce giant gooseberries amenable to our superficial terminology about first and second subjects almost until the beginning of the nineteenth century. There was, perhaps, a feeling

among persons of old-fashioned tastes that Haydn's regrettable
noisiness and love of caricature were producing a widespread
decline in musical civilization; but even our own shrewd Dr.
Burney, who died in 1814, recorded the most interesting conver-
sations with Gluck and Philipp Emanuel Bach, and yet showed
so little consciousness of the real revolution that had come over
music that he ranks as important developments 'the new ways of
taking *appoggiaturas* and notes of taste'. Burney's limitations seem
absurd to us, because time has shown that he failed to back the
winners; but most of our notions of musical form are quite as
superficial as Burney's, and after a century or two we happen to
know the names of the winners, simply because we have been
told. Whether a movement has one theme or half a dozen, whether
its texture is polyphonic or homophonic—all such questions tell
us as little about the real capacity of a work as the way in which
a horse's mane is clipped can tell us of its capacity on a race-course.

The essentials of the sonata style result in many ways of
development and many kinds of texture that would have been
inconceivable to Bach and Handel, but even these features do not
in a bird's-eye view of music reveal themselves as less superficial
than Burney's 'new ways of taking *appoggiaturas* and notes of
taste'. Important things in musical history can be learnt from a
bird's-eye view, just as photography from aeroplanes has revealed
unexpected and abundant traces of Roman camps, and even
Roman towns, which no study on the level of the ground could
ever discover; but what matters in the enjoyment of music is,
not the history, nor the bird's-eye view, but precisely the ground-
level view; and my complaint against most of our text-book
knowledge of musical form is just that it is all up in the clouds,
and distracts the listener's attention from everything which can
help him to listen to the music. Now, the essentially dramatic
quality of the music of Haydn, Mozart, and Beethoven is precisely
the quality which the listener can find present all the time. Even
in such merely symmetrical dance-forms as minuets and scherzos
without any codas or digressions, the tunes have a quality which
is not anticipated by Bach's lightest gavottes and other *Galan-
terien*. Of course, when the scale is so small and the form so
merely lyric, the dramatic quality of the things in themselves
cannot be more than subtleties; but these little minuets and
scherzos do not exist in themselves. They are dramatic by position. Nothing, for instance, can be more dramatic in this way
than the position of the tiniest of all, the middle movement of
the C sharp minor ('Moonlight') Sonata, op. 27, no. 2, which
Liszt finely described as '*une fleur entre deux abîmes*'.

We will not pursue subtleties any farther, but will now return
to our usual practice of taking the most vivid illustrations first.

The dramatic power of Beethoven has already been forcibly illustrated, and further examples of it will speak for themselves, not only as to their self-evident force, but as to their means of expression. The matter in which the listener is now likely to need most help is the very important principle that even the largest of sonata forms retains as a whole some of the qualities of a single melody. While this position at the breaking-point between lyric and drama has its own notorious difficulties, it accounts for the fact that the dramatic emotion of a style like Beethoven's is enormously more intense than anything that can be achieved by a less concentrated kind of music. The music moves at the pace of a short story, while its power of climax is that of a full-sized drama. Doubtless, to many readers and especially to many musicians, the statement that Beethoven is thus a more emotional artist than, say, Wagner, will seem a wilful paradox, but I must take leave here to save time by asserting that it is a reasoned truth which I am prepared to substantiate in forty volumes, while the denial of it comes from conventional habits of mind based on professional misinformation.

There are good grounds for the popular notion that Beethoven was a revolutionary in music. This notion dates from his own times, though, as a matter of fact, he was not more often attacked as a revolutionary than as a pedant who 'piled up masses of erudition without good method', a remark which I quote from an early review of Beethoven's first violin sonatas. It may be fruitful to regard Beethoven as revolutionary, and it may be fruitful to regard his methods as learned or naïve; but the central fact about all his art is that he never obliterated distinctions or obscured his purposes. Moreover, while his art devotes itself to the maintenance of interest from beginning to end, and therefore never 'gives away' his purpose too soon, he never leaves the listener in doubt about anything that it is necessary to know. The one important exception to this is in the work which gave him more trouble than anything else in his career, the opera *Fidelio*; and here the fault is in the libretto, which is really difficult to follow. I often refer to the case of *Fidelio*, for by its narrow escape from failure it will reveal aspects of the immense clarity of Beethoven's insight which we do not even take for granted, but accept without knowing of their existence.

The first feature that can present itself to us in any work of art is an introduction, but it will be more convenient to consider introductions after we have considered what they introduce, for the majority of Beethoven's works begin without introductions, and of his introductions only a small number are purely introductory. It would be absurd to call the west front of Peterborough Cathedral a mere introduction, when it is obviously the most impressive part of the building; and it would be not less absurd to see merely prefatory features in such huge designs as the introductions to the G minor Violoncello Sonata, op. 5, no. 2, and the Seventh Symphony. There is no necessity for us always to know from the outset whether a movement is going to stand alone or to introduce something else. But it is vitally necessary to know from the outset that an exposition is an exposition, and, if the exposition is going to deceive us about the kind of thing it is destined to expose, the composer must have a satisfactory explanation for the deception.

Shakespeare chooses to begin *Twelfth Night* with a piece of music. He does not write the music, but something must be played or sung and brought to a definite end, in order to explain the first spoken words: 'If music be the food of love, play on. . . . That strain again; it had a dying fall.' In this case, therefore, a lyric opening becomes the dramatic means of revealing the character of the sentimental Orsino. But it is not often that a drama can afford to begin with a lyric, and for the same reason it is not often that a movement full of active development can afford to begin with a square tune. Listeners whose fondness for melody has not risen far superior to my own sinful fondness for square tunes will find that their insight into Beethoven's larger designs will grow rapidly if they select those cases where Beethoven has begun a highly developed movement with a dangerously broad and symmetrical melody. Nothing can be more quiet than the way in which such a melody will disengage itself from symmetry and broaden into something evidently part of a larger whole; and the process is as dramatic as it is quiet. The two clearest instances are the openings of the first 'Rasoumovsky' Quartet (F major, op. 59, no. 1) and the B flat Trio, op. 97.

In the first eight bars of the F major Quartet you hear two splendid lines of melody in the violoncello. You expect another eight bars, and are not surprised when the answer begins on the dominant chord, though, as a matter of fact, the harmony has changed to dominant half a bar before you expected it. But try holding your breath until that dominant closes again into a tonic. For the rest, our studies of rhythm will have helped your natural capacity to appreciate the much shorter new phrases that follow. There is not a vestige of formal symmetry in the rest of the opening: neither is there anything which can be taken for discursive development. The sequence of events is dramatic, and their logic will appear in the retrospect when the whole movement is finished.

The opening of the B flat Trio, op. 97, takes the risk of rounding off its melody with some symmetry. One reason for this is that the pianoforte naturally forms one mass of harmony, while the violin and the violoncello form another, and this gives occasion for antiphonal correspondences; but the melody having reached a dominant close at the eighth bar, the violin and 'cello intervene quite dramatically with six bars of sustained declamatory dialogue, which removes all premature effect of symmetry from the counter-statement that now follows. A counterstatement is a restatement of an idea with a change of direction, and thus is eminently a device suitable for exposition—though it may hamper dramatic movement if it is too symmetrical. Here, however, apart from the intervention of those six bars of dialogue, the counterstatement broadens and deepens till no doubt of the dramatic scope of the music remains.

Ex 18.

In the Seventh Symphony, the tune at the beginning of the Vivace is more obviously a dance tune (and we may regard dance as a subspecies of lyric). Berlioz called it a '*ronde des paysans*', one of the silliest remarks a Latin demigod ever made about the denizens of Olympus, but not nearly so silly as the apologies that have been made for those tuneful elements in one of the mightiest of symphonies. Anything can be taken for anything else if you remove it from its context. The passage from the introduction into the Vivace is so obviously dramatic that in Beethoven's time it excited derision. Forget the rest of the introduction, play its last six bars, and continue for the first three and a half bars of the Vivace, and you will get something quite meaningless in itself. Similarly, you might take *King Lear* and quote from the scene of his death the three words 'Undo this button'. Those six expiring bars of introduction passing into the four bars of Vivace are in their context among the supreme dramatic achievements of Beethoven; and in their context the words 'Undo this button' are among the most overwhelming touches of Shakespeare's pathos. Thus, Beethoven's dance tune can afford to dance because of its context. Count the bars of the Vivace, and you will find that in bars 15 and 17 the symmetry is already broken by echoes. Even if there had been nothing dramatic in the way in which the tune was introduced, these irregularities have not come too late to prevent the drama from relapsing into pageantry. Less tuneful types of opening naturally leave us in less doubt about the dramatic quality of a movement, but they can afford to consist of architectural conventions rather than of individual ideas; and of all forms of criticism that is the most dangerous and most frequently futile which starts by laying down that a great piece of music must have pregnant original themes, and continues by comparing the merits of one theme with another on that assumption. It is impossible on such lines to prove that Spohr was not the greatest composer of his age, with Mendelssohn as his nearest rival. Nobody should attempt to criticize Beethoven until he has mastered two works which stultify this criterion once for all, the E flat Trio, op. 70, no. 2, and the so-called 'Harp' Quartet in E flat, op. 74. In the 'Harp' Quartet, the only theme which would seem to any composer but Beethoven pregnant enough to deserve a moment's attention is not developed at all; and in the E flat Trio, the first movement shocks all the wiseacres by re-discovering several of Mozart's favourite turns of phrase, and the second movement reveals a form peculiar to Haydn. It would be solemn impertinence to apologize for either of these works by saying that they make remarkable use of intrinsically unimportant themes. We must simply face the fact that our musical terminology is misleading, and that, if we even begin by taking themes for ideas, we shall end by missing all musical ideas whatever. The safe criterion is the principle already mentioned, that the sonata forms as wholes represent the conception of melody at a point at which it has expanded so as to cover the whole emotional range of a drama, while at the same time retaining its unity as melody. In short, form is melody writ large, and while much may be learnt by breaking forms up into themes, there are cases where you might as well expect to learn something of a drama by breaking it up into syllables.

If it is thus unsafe to criticize themes as things in themselves, it is for the same reason still more unsafe to rely upon the

connexion of one theme with another as providing a logical basis for
music, even where the connexion is obvious. Where it is not obvious,
the listener had much better not look for it. If the composer
wishes it to appear, he will sooner or later place his intention
beyond doubt to any one who is not deaf. Connexions visible only
to the eye are accidental, unless the composer has descended to
non-aesthetic regions of cryptography. In the third *Leonore* Overture, the supreme dramatic moment of the trumpet-call is followed by a wonderful new melody, which in the opera expresses
the awe-struck sense of deliverance. Grove ingeniously derived the
notes of this theme from those of the main theme of the Overture.
In order to do this, he had to ignore, or violently misconstrue,
its whole scheme of accents, and he had also to do without the
slightest vestige of support from Beethoven, who has not connected
the two ideas in any way that can appeal to the ear. Sometimes Beethoven's sketches show us that he had a connexion in his mind, and
that he got rid of it. A trap into which Grove fell with delightful
Irish simplicity is that of the first bars of the *Leonore* Overtures,
Nos. 2 and 3. The first overture that Beethoven wrote was the one
known as No. 2, and it begins with three slowly descending notes:

Ex.19

These were repeated and prolonged into a descending scale.
Performances of *Leonore* No. 2 are rare, because, though it has
extremely interesting features of its own, it is unquestionably
superseded by *Leonore* No. 3; so that Grove, like all concert-goers,
knew No. 3 first. Now, obviously, if you are to enjoy No. 2 on
its own merits, you must dismiss No. 3 from your mind. It is
no use imputing to Beethoven a spirit of prophecy. You must
take No. 2 as you find it. So taking it, you will see that it starts
with a figure of three notes, expands them into a scale, and then,
after mysterious modulations, turns that three-note figure into
the beautiful melody in A flat which, in the opera, becomes the
theme of Florestan's great aria in the dungeon scene. In *Leonore*
No. 3 this point has disappeared. The overture begins with a
long pause on the first of the three notes, and then proceeds
straight down the scale, so that all resemblance to Florestan's air
has vanished; but our delightful Grove, who in *Leonore* No. 3
sees with his eye resemblances which do not exist for the ear, can
neither see nor hear *Leonore* No. 2 without so prophetic a vision
of No. 3 that he calls its first three notes 'a false start'! Notice
that it is quite unnecessary that the long descending scale of
Leonore No. 3 should be a theme at all. It fixes the key of C major

from the dominant outwards and then falls upon an unexpected F sharp which sends us we know not whither. Then out of the intense darkness comes Florestan's air, which means all the more from not having been anticipated by a piece of thematic logic.

Do not, therefore, be surprised, or, if you enjoy the surprise, do not try to minimize it, by discovering clever logical connexions when Beethoven makes an exposition of several disconnected ideas thrown at you with Mozartean abruptness, as at the beginning of the E flat Sonata, op. 7, and the B flat Sonata, op. 22. Clever people tell us that in op. 7 the rhythmic figure of bars 1–4 is latent in the bass of bars 5–10. If you are as clever as all that, you may be far too clever to see that the right hand of bars 5–12 is not a single voice, but is in dialogue; that the C at the end of bar 6 goes down to the following B flat in the left hand, while a new voice answers the figure above; and that there is a similar new entry at the join of bars 8–9. These facts are not evident to the eye, but they are evident to the ear, unless the player has no natural instinct for phrasing. A composer who has written over a hundred works in sonata form cannot fail to have procedures that can be classified; yet there is little use in attempting the classification of Beethoven's expositions. It is natural that he should more often begin with a business-like bundle of agenda than with a broad melody that has a tendency to become lyrical. Throughout his life, Beethoven was dealing with forms that had just become capable of vast new developments. We may impute this capacity to the forms themselves without prejudice to the pious opinion that nobody but Beethoven could have seen their capacity for development. Probably it was the new possibilities that left him small leisure to produce many openings consisting of architectural formulas, such as those so common, and often so important, in Mozart. The Allegro of the First Symphony is a case in point, and we have already contrasted its dryly architectural treatment of the supertonic and the subdominant with the quiet melodic breadth of the opening of the C major Quintet, op. 29. This contrast is the more instructive because the architectural formalities take up far more room than the melody: so much so that Beethoven can repeat the whole melody at once, whereas his architectural opening has taken up all the available space. On the other hand, it is interesting to see that the business aspect of Beethoven's dramatic style is a feature of nature which is bound to return, in spite of all efforts of lyric melody to pitchfork it out of sight. The next step in the action of the C major Quintet is quite as dry and formal as anything in the First Symphony. Moreover, though convenient, it is not quite correct to regard a Mozartean architectural opening as merely architectural. On the contrary, most of its formulas were originally dramatic. The formula with which the so-called 'Jupiter' Symphony opens is the cliché for the gesture of the tyrant on his throne brandishing his sceptre while the humble suppliant pleads at his feet. It would be a mistake to read the original dramatic import of the cliché into Mozart's architectural opening: the intelligent lover of architecture need not distress himself at the thought of the agonies of the Caryatides sustaining their loads. There is aesthetic pleasure in the fact that such figures have become formulas. It is a great and divine honour to become a formula, and it is entirely in accordance with this that some of Beethoven's most architectural openings are also his most dramatic; it is impossible to begin either more architecturally or more dramatically than the *Sonata Appassionata.*

Do not look for any rule to govern the number of themes in Beethoven's expositions. In the exposition of the Sonata, op. 2, no. 1, there is only one theme; there are three in op. 2, no. 2; and at least two in op. 2, no. 3. The question soon becomes ambiguous, for no exposition in music or literature can indefinitely delay the point at which a transition to something new becomes necessary. Our English terminology, having misnamed the exposition of a sonata the 'first subject', must needs call the something new the 'second subject', and of all futilities musical lore has nothing more futile than controversies about where the second subject begins or which of its various themes deserves that title. The listener will do well to rest content with his own impressions whether something new is happening. It is worth while his taking pains to develop his sense of key-relation, because the first essential dramatic action that follows upon the exposition of the first group is the establishment of a new key, and by establishment I mean, not merely the footing on which Bach's and Handel's keys will visit their neighbours, but a process by which the home tonic has definitely passed beyond the horizon. For what happens in the new key, there are no rules binding on any composers greater than our now despised and neglected Hummel, Clementi, and Spohr. Even Clementi is capable of commendable freedom, while Mendelssohn's apparently classical facility is as unconsciously sceptical as the alleged advice of the latitudinarian bishop to 'look the difficulties boldly in the face and pass on'.

Counting the themes in any large second group is as troublesome as counting the sentences in a chapter of prose: if a writer is as fond of colons as I am, some estimates may give twice as many sentences as others: and the punctuation of Victorian maiden aunts and of A. P. Herbert's adorable Lady Topsy Haddock produces an aesthetically valuable effect of continuity by being severely restricted to commas. Musical punctuation derives a

further continuity when there is enough polyphony for one part
to run on across the articulations of another. Such complexity
I have purposely refrained from analysing. It is no source of
confusion; on the contrary, the articulations become the more
cogent the more means we have of diversifying them. Obviously,
the full stop at which all the elements unite is more emphatic
when it stands in contrast to articulations that have not blocked
the undercurrents.

Now let us look at some of Beethoven's transitions from his
first group to his second. The orthodox view of his early style is
that it shows the influence of Haydn and Mozart and follows
their practice. Influences are dangerous red herrings to draw over
the trail of a work of art if we wish to carry out the artist's aim
by enjoying the work as a thing in itself. It would be idle to
deny the influence of Haydn and Mozart upon Beethoven at
almost any period of his career. And it is hardly less interesting
to trace the influence of Philipp Emanuel Bach, of Cherubini,
and of composers who are now forgotten. But it is much more
interesting and important to note that almost the majority of
Beethoven's early works show a nervous abruptness which is as
different from the humour of Haydn as it is from the Olympic
suavity of Mozart. There are, indeed, early works which are
Mozartean, notably the most brilliant success of Beethoven's first
period, the Septet, which is perhaps the only work of Beethoven's
which earned Haydn's unqualified and enthusiastic praise; but
the Mozartean Beethoven imitates only the lighter side of Mozart.
In the Quintet for pianoforte and wind instruments, op. 16,
Beethoven is, indeed, obviously setting himself in rivalry with
Mozart's Quintet for the same combination; but, if you want to
realize the difference between the highest art of classical composition and the easy-going, safety-first product of a silver age,
you cannot find a better illustration than these two works, and
here it is Mozart who is the classic and Beethoven who is something less. The real influence of Mozart and Haydn was slow to
show itself in Beethoven's style, and what did eventually appear
was the integration of Mozart's and Haydn's resources, with
results that transcend all possibility of resemblance to the style
of their origins, and are nowhere more transcendent than in a
work like the E flat Trio, op. 70, no. 2, where Beethoven discovers
new meanings for Mozart's phrases and Haydn's formulas. In
the construction of sonatas, as of dramas, the transition, or the
first decisive step in the action, is perhaps more difficult than any
other part of the art problem, and in Beethoven's early works the
difficulty appears in the fact that the transitions are often extraordinarily clever, and sometimes very roundabout. In a loosely
constructed work, Beethoven is not above using an old Italian

practical joke which Mozart often used in his slighter works. The joke consists in letting the exposition reach a pause on the home dominant, and then, like Mr. Wemmick in *Great Expectations*, saying: 'Hulloa, here's a church! Let's go in! . . . Let's have a wedding!'—in other words, treating this home dominant as a real key and continuing in it. Probably Nature, having been driven out with a pitchfork, will assert herself by introducing the necessary enhanced dominant at a later stage, just as Mr. Wemmick was certainly able to produce the necessary documents in time for the wedding to proceed.

In the Sonata, op. 2, no. 3, the practical joke is followed by the remarkable passage which Beethoven resurrected from one of his juvenile pianoforte quartets, a passage which, starting in the dominant minor, roams through several keys on a systematically falling bass. In the First Symphony, Beethoven takes no trouble after his practical joke. The opening theme of the second group has its own modulations to its dominant, and that is not what we mean by establishing the key through its enhanced dominant. This is no mistake on Beethoven's part. It simply means that in the First Symphony Beethoven is content with the lighter dramatic values of comedy of manners. In the opening of the A major Sonata, op. 2, no. 2, a formidable Beethovenish energy is ready to break out through the architectural formulas. In the transition and preparation for the second group, Beethoven attains a grandly classical breadth. The second group has already been quoted as a *locus classicus* for his most powerful handling of the rising bass in wide modulations. It is one of the strangest vagaries of criticism that has allowed this epoch-making work to be overshadowed by the outwardly more pretentious Sonata in C, op. 2, no. 3. If Beethoven's early works had been mostly in the style of opus 2, no. 3, or of the Violoncello Sonata in F, op. 5, no. 1, and he had died before producing anything more characteristic, it would have been possible to argue that here was an ambitious composer who evidently aspired to be greater than either Mozart or Haydn, but who already showed the tendency to inflation that leads through the style of Hummel to the degenerate styles of the virtuoso pianoforte-writers. We could even point to the cadenzas in the first movements of opus 2, no. 3, and opus 5, no. 1, and in the finale of the Septet, as illustrations of a licence which was beneath the dignity of Haydn and Mozart. In the light of Beethoven's actual record, we need not view these lapses so severely as Beethoven doubtless viewed them himself. The mature Beethoven had seen the folly of them all. We may even be glad to allow the young Beethoven to see the folly of just three; and, as a matter of fact, cadenza-writing is a very good exercise in composition, and these are good cadenzas. Still, it is not

for these things that we need to study Beethoven's early
works.

There is more to be learnt from his early nervous abruptness.
One of the most illuminating ways of listening to classical music
is to ignore all your previous information and to let the music
tell you step by step whether it is the work of a master; or, if
that be a question-begging term, whether it is meant to be a
sustained effort of composition. Any provocative young man can
throw at your head a formula, an epigram, or a paradox. You
are told that a work is a sonata. This is as much as to say that
it is a novel or drama. The curtain rises or the book opens upon
the now proverbial sentence: ' "Hell!" said the Duchess,' etc.
This is promising as far as it goes, but it does not of itself assure
us that the author can develop to good dramatic purpose the
conversation in which the Duchess had hitherto from modesty
taken no part. Epigrammatists are much less rare than dramatists.
A young artist who is capable of drama is almost certainly capable
of epigram, and his dramatic instincts must be powerful if he is
to resist the temptation of sacrificing them to the easier art of
epigram. There is an opposite source of dramatic weakness, and
that is what is shown in certain features of the Sonatas, op. 2,
no. 3, and op. 5, no. 1, the Septet, and the Quintet for
pianoforte and wind. Luxurious and loosely constructed as these
works are, they might have led to a degeneration into something
like the master of the well-constructed play. Here, again, my own
private conviction is that it is ungrateful to spend much of one's
critical life in grumbling at things which give refined pleasure.
Only professional critics are obliged to take an overdose of them,
and if the epigrammatist succeeds in distending himself into a
writer of well-constructed plays, we may pity the hard fate of the
forcibly fed critic without being ungrateful to the eupeptic
dramatist who gives us as much pleasure as we choose to accept
at his hands. Beethoven himself can afford to be made of sterner
stuff. The C minor Sonata, op. 10, no. 1, shows a nervousness
which seems out of proportion to the subject-matter. Being in a
minor key, the sonata is in a peevish, but not a tragic, temper, and
it begins with a tonic-and-dominant formula. Except that the
gestures are impatient, there is nothing here that need make
Beethoven less Olympic than the Mozart of the C minor Pianoforte Sonata and the C minor Octet for wind instruments (which
is better known in its version as a string quintet). But there is
already a subtlety in Beethoven's first theme. By the time its
pathetic continuation has come to a close broken by decidedly
dramatic pauses, it is evident that the step of the rhythm has
changed. There are analysts so clever that they tell us that the
very first bar of the sonata was an anacrusis, but Beethoven does

not write for listeners with a spirit of prophecy or armed with stop-watches which will tell them that a gun has been fired one second before it was due. We ordinary beings for whom the angelic Beethoven writes find it easier to assume that the initial bump is the beginning of the music, and that somewhere, no matter where, the rhythm has changed step during the pathetic continuation. Not only does this account represent what we actually hear, but, if you try to give any other interpretation to the main theme, you will find it violently contradicted every time that theme returns. Be this as it may, the first group of this sonata is abrupt. The transition, on the other hand, is profoundly thoughtful; beginning with what might be an epigram, it passes into dominant preparations admirable in their classic breadth, and the second group for ever settles the question whether this sonata is a continuous composition. The discussion of Beethoven's slow movements must come later, but here it is relevant to observe that neither the very impressive Largo appassionato of the A major Sonata, op. 2, no. 2, nor the Adagio of this little C minor Sonata, shows that Beethoven as yet feels ready to attempt a powerful design in a slow tempo. In opus 2, no. 2, the slow movement is solemn, and in opus 10, no. 1, it is melodious; but in neither case does it attempt to be more than sectional in its total effect, except perhaps at the end of that in the C minor Sonata, where the coda, with the evident attempt at an effect of breadth, becomes dangerously thin. It was not long before Beethoven found out that what such a coda needed was, not to expand itself, but to make the rest of the movement seem gigantic by introducing a human detail in the foreground. He already achieves this in the last line in the slow movement of the *Sonata Pathétique*, and we have described one of the finest and most surprising of all such devices in the last line of the slow movement of the D minor Sonata, op. 31, no. 2.

The finale of opus 10, no. 1, is violently compressed. Properly played, it sounds broader than one might expect. This finale is the first of two occasions on which Beethoven used the direction 'prestissimo' for a whole movement, the other case being in the second movement of the Sonata, op. 109. In both cases the direction is unfortunate. A player experienced in Beethoven's style will soon find that in the effort to be clear in the details of these highly compressed and highly charged movements one is apt to drag. As a warning against this tendency, the direction 'prestissimo' is natural enough, but as a positive direction to players whose ideas of classical style are vague, it is very misleading. When such music is played as fast as possible, it gives no more impression of pace than a sewing-machine. If it is really to sound fast, you must hear what it says.

Now turn to the next sonata, the F major, op. 10, no. 2. Here is Beethoven the epigrammatist at his wittiest, and on paper the finale looks more violently compressed than that of opus 10, no. 1; but the two works are in quite different categories. There is no conflict in opus 10, no. 2. The epigrams of the first movement are abrupt enough. Beethoven effects the transition (as he had already done more broadly in his first Sonata, op. 2, no. 1) by pretending to move in quite a different direction. The orthodox enhanced dominant afterwards asserts itself clearly enough; but throughout the whole first movement and finale Beethoven is at ease because the style is thoroughly humorous. Humour, as the modern psychologists tell us, is a defensive instinct, and it is not surprising that it should prove rather a solvent of elements that might otherwise incite to pugnacity. The middle movement enlarges and completes the scope of the whole sonata by means of deep pathos; and being purely lyric in form, practically a minuet and trio, it has none of the responsibilities of a slow movement with a large design.

In the D major Sonata, op. 10, no. 3, Beethoven's power appears with an intensity which must have come more as a shock than as a revelation to his contemporaries. It is doubtful whether any part of it except the exquisite minuet can have been acceptable to orthodox musicians in 1798. The slow movement is not only Beethoven's first essay in tragedy, but is by far the most tragic piece of music that had ever been written up to that time. In the recent, but now moribund, reaction against Romanticism, some of our cleverest writers achieve their best effects of unconscious comedy by casting doubts upon its sincerity. They should know better than to mistake for insincerity that early phase of technique in which the artist has recourse to carefully measured pauses that are dangerous rhetorical gestures, or stage effects. The occasion for such effects is adequate, and their danger is nothing compared with that of filling up their spaces with explanations. They are not so abnormal in opus 10, no. 3, as to destroy the continuity of the design; and still less do they overstrain the suggestive powers of the pianoforte and the listener's capacity to integrate slow broken rhythms, as happens in the slow movement of the Sonata, op. 7, where Beethoven is evidently working at high emotional pressure. If such things are defects, they are signs of excitement, not of insincerity. Even in his early works, Beethoven indulges in rhetorical gestures and pauses less often than Haydn, and then only for Haydn's reasons—that it is better to break off than to explain. It is interesting to compare the slow movement of opus 10, no. 3, with two later slow movements in the same key: the Adagio of the F major String Quartet, op. 18, no. 1, and the Largo of the D major Trio, op. 70, no. 1. In all three movements the return to the home tonic after the development is measured in exact rhythmic terms, but is expressed with something like a pause. In opus 10, no. 3, the broken rhythms, two bars before the return of the theme, so entirely avoid any accented beat that they are quite difficult to follow. In opus 18, no. 1, the pauses lie between no less than four chords, each on the first beat of a very long bar. The proportion of silence thus becomes enormous. In opus 70, no. 1, the single bar which stops the rhythm contains two cadential chords, and the 'cello sings a sustained tenor dominant throughout. The result has none of the startling effect of the earlier examples, but is incalculably more impressive.

Turn now to the rest of the Sonata, op. 10, no. 3. The opening of the first movement seems to spring out at us like a panther. Beethoven, however, is an experienced sportsman with a camera instead of a gun. He has had to move his tripod too quickly to take a very continuous film, and we also had better abandon our metaphor and, descending to the musical plane, remark that Beethoven, after a pause for breath if not for safety, answers his first four bars with six bars, in themselves an expansion, but cut off with a full close. This still leaves his opening in the condition of the novel which begins with the famous objurgation of the otherwise retiring Duchess; and Beethoven sees that it would be futile to make anything else of the situation. He begins a counter-statement in which the panther springs just one step farther and knocks us into the middle of the next day. We might almost as well have said 'next week', for the next key is the so-called 'relative minor', and Beethoven needs a very long and flowing paragraph, passing through several keys, before he can arrive at his objective, the orthodox dominant; but this paragraph flows gloriously. Even apart from its context, it would be evidently the work of an artist with unlimited talent for composition, and in its context it justifies Beethoven for having begun his story with such alarming abruptness.

The Finale of the Sonata is in a peculiar case. We seem to have got over the anti-romantic reaction against Beethoven's slow movements, but fashionable criticism does not yet seem to have discovered Beethoven's sense of humour. I have already, almost unnecessarily, pointed out that critics are to be pitied, rather than reviled, for this omission, inasmuch as to describe Beethoven's humour adds to the horrors of all verbal description of music the hideous ineptitude of analysing jokes. Fortunately, as has been often pointed out, there is nothing which we fear so intensely as the accusation of not seeing the humour of this or that; so I shall confidently assert that Beethoven is humorous wherever I think that he is, and the reader may doubt me at his peril. The finale of opus 10, no. 3, is one of the funniest things Beethoven ever wrote, and differs from later and larger manifestations of his humour in the fact that it is not yet stated, like, for instance, the Finale of the Eighth Symphony, on an Olympian architectural scale.

Strange to say, it is neither in a tragedy nor in a formidably energetic work, but in one of the gentlest of his early comedies, that Beethoven keeps us longest in doubt whether the epigrammatist is going to reveal himself as a master of continuous form and architectural power. The G major Quartet, op. 18, no. 2, was at one time known as 'The Compliments', because its delicious opening theme was supposed to resemble some courtly person making a bow at the outset of a conversation. The conversation in this case is continued entirely in epigrams and in two-bar rhythm, so that the mere fact that the second group begins with an 8-bar phrase (4 + 4) passes for quite a notable broadening; but then this 8-bar tune is a counterstatement, and the continuation flows. The development section is quite profound and will well repay our attention when we study that aspect of musical form. It is interesting to find, in so quiet a comedy, Beethoven as nervous and jerky as if he had never heard of such achievements as his own G major Sonata, op. 14, no. 2. I can find no instances of nervous abruptness in any of Beethoven's second groups, and it would probably be safe to conclude that, if a composer or dramatist has not got some smoothness into his dramatic action after the first change of scene and the first change of outlook, he never will be more than an epigrammatist or an effect-maker. The difficulty of making a smooth transition at this stage of a movement has, as we have seen, produced in Beethoven's early works the paradox that, with few exceptions, his transitions are extraordinarily clever and roundabout, if they are not merely abrupt. If he had been content, like Hummel, to become an inflated Mozart with an over-fondness for glittering passages in the newly extended upper regions of the pianoforte, normal transition passages would have been the rule in his early works. Even so, they are not easy to write. Hummel and Spohr seem to do them easily because they are very considerable masters. Schubert, an artist of the highest genius who did not live to produce any but early works, almost always makes his transition by a *coup de théâtre* such as Beethoven would certainly have thought too crude, though it is as well, even with Schubert, to take such things on their own merits and not to be ungrateful for their effectiveness. The *locus classicus* for a Schubert transition is that in the first movement of the 'Unfinished' Symphony. Beethoven never cut his Gordian knot by a formal full close in the tonic followed by a three-bars' measured pause and cadence into the new key.

Though it is futile to count the number of themes in Beethoven's second groups, or to generalize about their relation to the first group, there is one phenomenon which Beethoven took over from Haydn and Mozart, called in German the *Schlussgruppe* and in English the cadence theme. It consists in a neat little phrase, new or old, which clearly asserts the cadential chords of the key of the group, and so marks this section off from the development which follows. We have no reason to call it a third subject or an xth subject, for, as we have already seen, the term 'subject' is an utter misnomer for sonata themes. With Haydn, it is often the only portion of his exposition which becomes clearly recapitulated at the end of the movement. It may not amount to a theme at all. In the first movement of the *Sonata Appassionata*, the five bars 61–65 fulfil the purpose of a cadence theme by merely asserting cadential chords three times. In the first movement of the 'Eroica' Symphony, the crowd of themes that constitutes the largest second group in all symphonic music ends with a single four-bar phrase, which may or may not be derived from previous material, that question being of no importance whatever so long as we understand the information the phrase intends to give us. In effect, it says: 'And that's that', trusting to the naïve listener to know what is what.

DEVELOPMENT

THE word 'development' has in music its ordinary dictionary meaning, but it also has a special meaning of the development section of a sonata movement. In whatever sense we use the word, we must still retain our grasp of the fact that the sonata style is essentially dramatic. In the ordinary sense of the word, the development of an idea is the unfolding of its possibilities. When you buy of a street-hawker a little packet of Japanese paper pellets, and drop them into a glass of water, they develop—that is to say, they unfold and become charming little flowers. Similarly, if Bach writes a piece of triple counterpoint—that is to say, a harmony made of three melodies, any one of which can become bass to the other two—he can develop these few bars into a good-sized fugue by exposing first one subject in three or four voices, then another, then the third, and, finally, by combining all three and giving as much as he chooses of their six possible permutations and combinations. Again, apart from the inversions or permutations of double and triple counterpoint, fugue-subjects can be melodically inverted in themselves—that is to say, there may be good musical sense in a version of the subject in which every rise is represented by an equal fall and vice versa. Then there are the devices of augmentation and diminution, by which the theme is stated twice as slowly or twice as fast. All these devices may prolong and diversify the development of a fugue-subject into an entire fugue. They may also be of some use in the treatment of sonata material. But it is fairly obvious that they are not dramatic developments. They have the same place in drama, and the same need for severe restriction, as philosophic arguments. From the vast regions of sonata style they are banished as rigorously as philosophy is from drama, and musical criticism, especially of the later works of Beethoven and of many aspects of the style of Brahms, is often nervously preoccupied with doubts whether Beethoven is legitimate in his attempts to fuse the styles of sonata and fugue.

The childish solution of this question consists in relying on the admitted and obvious fact that in natural talent for counterpoint there is no comparison between Beethoven and Mozart or Haydn; but neither is there any comparison between the natural contrapuntal talent of our severest doctors of music and that of Beethoven. Beethoven once said to that excellent and undeservedly forgotten English musician, Cipriani Potter: 'I have not studied enough.' Every great artist feels that at one time or another, though few are so likely to feel it as Beethoven, who throughout his life was inventing an appreciably new technique for almost every work he produced. On the other hand, Beethoven had no very high opinion of the difficulties of writing an academic fugue, and at no period of his career does he show the slightest roughness or awkwardness in handling counterpoint on familiar themes. The magnificent Overture *Die Weihe des Hauses* is throughout on a typical pair of classical fugue-themes in double counterpoint. It is a work of immense energy and has not a vestige of roughness or awkwardness. Again, the occasional displays of counterpoint in Beethoven's early works are far more than merely competent. They are, unquestionably, brilliant. They are not as unostentatious as Mozart's, and they are not meant to be, for Beethoven never released himself from his task of increasing his dramatic range; but take the triple counterpoint that adorns the recapitulation of the *Andante scherzoso quasi allegretto* in the C minor Quartet, op. 18, No. 4. If our masters of counterpoint have any criteria according to which that is not masterly, their criteria must lie outside anything we want to know about classical music. Further discussion of Beethoven's counterpoint as such belongs to a later chapter, but we must already beware of confusing the question of its intrinsic qualities as counterpoint with the general musical and dramatic question of the limits to the use of contrapuntal devices in sonata style and of explicit philosophic argument in drama. This parallel between music and drama is exact. The danger of a passage of fugue in a sonata is that it stops the action, just as a philosophic discussion may stop the action of a drama. On the other hand, if you follow most of our polyphonophobes in condemning such passages *a priori*, you will deprive music of exactly what you will deprive drama of, by a similar conscientious objection to discussion on the stage. Discussion may be a tensely dramatic form of action, and in Beethoven's sonata-works an outbreak of fugue is the ultimate incandescence of his drama; but the normal processes of development in the sonata style have nothing to do with fugue, and the fugal methods of transforming subjects are not developments, even according to the standards of fugue itself. The only aspect of a fugue which corresponds to development in the sense now in question is the episodes: those passages which are concerned, not with entries of a whole subject, but with sequences derived from its figures and the figures of its countersubjects. The merit of such developments consists in the varieties of phrase obtained from these sequences. A dull development will tell us, like one of Barry Pain's most cruel caricatures, that 'the inevitable consequences then followed, as they so often do'. A good development makes new melodies from old. In the article *Melody* in the

Encyclopaedia Britannica[1] I have given illustrations of this from
Beethoven, Wagner, and Brahms. Two things should be noted
at this point: first, that the listener must never forget the warning
that he is to trust his ear only, and not his eye. It will do him no
harm if he fails to hear all that is there; but if ocular analysis has
once begun to induce him to believe in unreal resemblances, he
will soon lose all capacity to appreciate real ones. The second
point is that the things Beethoven wishes to be heard are always
in juxtaposition. His process is evidently that of breaking up a
melody into small figures and rearranging these figures in
sequences. From this we may infer: first, that it is folly to talk
as if Beethoven's melody is built up of the small figures. It quite
evidently exists as a large idea, and the breaking up into small
figures is a means of producing, not smaller ideas, but ideas with
the cumulative power of sequences, a cumulative power which
the melody, as such, lacks. Secondly, we may infer that a theme
which itself consisted mainly of sequences will be less capable of
development. One very brilliant teacher of composition has,
quite rightly, tried to impress upon his pupils the necessity of
constructing long-breathed themes which contain several figures
before they repeat themselves; but he has fallen into the indis-
cretion of classifying themes as strong, when they are so constructed, and as weak, when they consist already of sequential
repetitions. What is true is that the themes which consist of
sequences have obviously exhausted most of their capacity for
development in their first statement. But what is development,
that it should arrogate to itself the right of determining whether
a theme is strong or weak? On this criterion, we are confronted
with the absurdity that Beethoven's weakest sequences are
those of the D minor Sonata and the *Coriolanus* Overture.
What is quite true is that in neither of these works do the
development sections differ markedly in texture from the rest.
Why should they?

We shall not make much progress in the understanding of
Beethoven or any other artist until we have got rid of the childish
notion that even the intellectual values of an art-form, apart from
its emotional content, can be measured by the ostensible intel-
lectuality of its devices. Yet many clever writers disappoint us
by falling into this booby-trap. One of the best modern books on
Mozart remarks upon the shortness of his developments: a quite
sound observation if it were not put forward as a weakness in an
otherwise almost perfect artist. Such criticism is quite incapable
of dealing with composition. Mozart's developments are usually
short, but they are invariably powerful, even when they seem to

---

[1] Now reprinted in *Musical Articles from the Encyclopaedia Britannica*, by
Donald Francis Tovey. Oxford University Press.

disclaim all responsibility for working out the themes of the exposition, and devote themselves to episodic matter instead. The question whether a development is adequate is not to be settled by cataloguing what it contains, but by finding out what it supports in the rest of the structure: in other words, by seeing whether it succeeds in producing a kind of phrasing the interest of which has not been exhausted in the exposition. A development that thus contrasts with the exposition will by the same means throw the recapitulation into welcome relief.

Turn again to the D minor Sonata, op. 31, no. 2. The main bulk of the first movement is occupied by sequential passages on a rising bass. It is permissible to regard the second group as beginning with the pregnant new figures of bars 41–54, though this is of the nature of dominant preparation, and the key of the tonic of A minor does not effectively appear until bar 55. Here again, what we have is a theme consisting of interlocking self-repetitions, capable of an expanded counterstatement by means of a dramatic digression, but certainly not capable of anything that could be properly called development. What then does Beethoven achieve after the double-bar in the section properly called development, or working out, which separates the exposition from the recapitulation? He satisfies the first need of a development by striking out into an unascertainably distant key. (I will deal later with the special issues raised by the changes of tempo in this movement.) In this remote key he begins his rising bass, and carries it on till it reaches the home dominant. We may thus call it developed, in the sense that it has fetched a wider compass; but when he reaches the home dominant he spends no less than 22 bars on it without any theme at all, and this is exactly what gives his development its full power.

The case of the *Coriolanus* Overture is more subtle, and though I had always understood it as a masterpiece of absolute music long before I had an opportunity of reading Collin's very un-Shake-spearean play, I have been able to describe the music much more easily in the light of what Beethoven happened to be illustrating than in purely musical terms. Teachers of composition usually frown upon merely episodic developments—that is to say, developments which abandon the themes of the exposition and indulge in irresponsible new ideas. But it is absurd to talk as if a composer invented new episodes in order to save himself trouble. In fact, it is much easier to be clever with themes already given than to be prolific with new ones. Perhaps the most difficult of all things to get exactly right are such themeless passages as those 22 bars before the recapitulation in the D minor Sonata.

In the first movement of the little E major Sonata, op. 14, no. 1, Beethoven definitely spent more pains in avoiding cleverness than

in displaying it. In the second group, the self-repeating figure of
bars 39/40 was originally identical with the figure of bar 4, but
Beethoven carefully obliterated the allusion. Most of the development is occupied by a long-drawn episode in A minor. It may be
wise to forbid a young composer any such episodic indulgence,
but they are not things that a person can do by inadvertence.
Beethoven's sketch-book shows that at this point he made a note
to the effect: Don't develop the theme. The young composer
should be warned, not that such indulgences are vicious, but that,
before he can risk them, he must learn to do more obviously
clever things.

Beethoven had before him two great and diametrically opposite
classical methods of development. Mozart, whether he is episodic
or highly intellectual and contrapuntal, almost always concen-
trates his development section in one process, which goes through
a more or less wide range of keys (an extreme range in both the
first movement and the finale of the G minor Symphony), and
returns to the home tonic with just enough dominant preparation
to lead to the recapitulations with an effect of royal punctuality.
It is very rare for a Mozart development to contain more than one
process. It is equally rare for a mature development by Haydn
to contain less than two; in quite a number of important cases
Haydn takes the utterly subversive course of casually returning
to the home tonic with his main theme fairly early in the course
of the development. University authorities do not look with
favour upon the undergraduate who turns up in vacation time
when no arrangements exist for a long-vacation term; nor has
Haydn the slightest intention of organizing any such arrangements. This unexpected return is a mere occasion for a much
more adventurous development. It is like the device of a conjuror
who, having shown you a fairly simple trick, proceeds, under
pretence of showing you how it was done, to display a series of
much more surprising tricks. Eventually, Haydn comes to the
real return, and this time he will have a more or less Mozartean
preparation, to ensure that it shall be expected, although the
external features of his style are naïve enough to permit him
sometimes to strike an attitude with a pause, a thing which Mozart
never does, and which Beethoven did with some subtlety for the
last time in the first movement of the Sonata, op. 28.

Beethoven's works show every conceivable kind of development, and from the vast material that claims our attention it will
perhaps be most profitable to select what is necessarily the main
dramatic point in any development: the return to the home
tonic for purposes of recapitulation. Neither Haydn nor Mozart
was able to make this return a highly emotional feature. Haydn's
premature return early in his development is humorous, and its

sequel in a swing-out to further adventures reveals the humour. Such are the limits of its dramatic force. Mozart never makes a sudden return, and the utmost effect that he obtains by any unusual delay is an effect of dignity and breadth; but in Beethoven's more important works it is not easy to think of a return that is not positively exciting, and he has no stereotyped device for producing the excitement. I have already cited the crescendo on the home dominant in the 'Waldstein' Sonata, the similar but far more exciting crescendo on the home tonic in the Fourth Symphony, and the terrible tragic climax in the first movement of the *Sonata Appassionata*. These are examples of tense expectation. Turn to the E flat major Trio, op. 70, no. 2, (see Ex. 16, p. 53) and you will find that in the course of a short development the instruments are happily conversing over the Mozartean main theme of the second group in various remote keys, when suddenly their attention is directed to the first figure of the main theme. The harmony stands poised on a chord that impinges upon the home dominant. This we can hardly expect to recognize as such, and, as a matter of fact, the bass then steps a tone downwards into another dominant, that of D flat ($\flat$VII), which lies quite in the opposite direction. In that key, nevertheless, the 'cello bursts out *forte* with the main theme, and is promptly corrected by the pianoforte in the home tonic; from which point the recapitulation proceeds with an air of noticing nothing unusual. This is perhaps the most unexpected return in all music. It is, in fact, a sudden return in the wrong key, promptly pulled round into the right key.

If the main theme should happen to begin with some other chord than that of the tonic, there will always be a dramatic subtlety in its return, for the composer is unlikely to lose the opportunity of preparing a return to the chord itself, without telling us too much about its key. At all events, one can hardly imagine a composer showing so little sense of his opportunities as to prepare for an ordinary return to the home tonic with the purpose of closing therein and starting again. Thus, for instance, in the E flat Sonata, op. 31, no. 3, the first chord of the main theme is that known as an added sixth: a very good name, inasmuch as, if you take a triad upon the subdominant and add a sixth to it, this chord will result. When theorists tell us that it is really a chord of the dominant eleventh which has happened to omit the dominant and the third, they are evidently saying 'the thing that is not', especially at the opening of this sonata, where the whole point is that the bass starts on the subdominant and gradually moves up towards the dominant. The chord is this or that, according to the way in which it happens. Why should it not be a chord of the added fifth—that is to say, a sixth into which a fifth has crept? That is what happens at the end of the development. Beethoven finds himself on a sixth in the key of F minor. Its top note happens to be the right note for the main theme. Beethoven plays about with the chord, sings the figure of the theme on it, and, at the third bar of the recapitulation thus begun, inserts the missing fifth.

The finale of the great B flat Trio, op. 97, is a marvellous study in Bacchanalian indolence. The theme begins in the subdominant (that is to say, its tonic is dominant to the subdominant), and it makes very little effort to maintain its proper balance against this bias. Even its second group hardly succeeds in establishing more than the home dominant, without any enhanced dominant to give the orthodox effect of the dominant key, and whenever the main theme returns, the warning necessarily takes the form of preparation for the subdominant. It is true that a diminished seventh interposes a faint cloud-veil over the procedure, but who minds what a diminished seventh says? With still further effrontery, the middle episode chooses to begin in the subdominant, and modulates only to nearly-related keys. Again, there is the warning of return to our main theme; but now comes a final effrontery, namely, that our little second group, which only succeeded in maintaining itself on, and not in, the dominant, is now recapitulated, not only in the subdominant, but with particular emphasis upon the subdominant's own subdominant chord. A belated apology is made for this by repeating the main second-group theme in the home tonic, but then we have for the last time the warning of a return to the main theme. The cloudy diminished seventh is present, and this time we are compelled to listen to it, for it changes its meaning and takes us into a remoter key than those mapped out in the gorgeous key-system of the other three movements.

The finale of the E minor Quartet, op. 59, no. 2, entirely satisfies us that, like the rest of the quartet, its tonic is E, but it insists on beginning in C major, with a theme that repeats itself many times. In the rest of this movement, the question of a return will arise. What is it that will return, the key of E minor or the key of the theme? If the key of the theme, then, the more we prepare for its return, the less we shall prepare for the return of E minor. As the movement proceeds, we begin to recognize that a return to C major is the shortest way home. Beethoven does not take the trouble to prove to us that a return to E minor would, if followed by his main theme in that key, probably lead us far astray.

The reader can perhaps best estimate the full range of Beethoven's dramatic power by comparing the returns in four of the largest movements Beethoven ever wrote. The first movement of

the 'Eroica' Symphony ends the longest of all Beethoven's developments with the longest of all his passages of anticipation. In the
first movement of the Ninth Symphony an already long and spacious
development has settled down to a quiet conversation which shows
no sign that anything will disturb its gentle pathos, until quite
suddenly the heavens are on fire and the foundations of the earth
are shaken. The introduction with which the movement had
begun so mysteriously on a bare fifth is now heard in the full
orchestra with a terribly ironic major harmony, that soon gives
way to the D minor of the titanic main theme. Thirdly, in the
Overture *Leonore*, No. 3, the development has covered enough
ground for ordinary formal purposes when it is dramatically
arrested by the trumpet-call behind the stage: a device which one
of our most brilliant critics has quoted as evidence of Beethoven's
inability to concentrate upon the essentials of form. The stage,
however, has its own essentials of musical form, and *Leonore*,
No. 3, happens to be a piece of stage music. Apart from this,
there is no reason why distance should not be allowed its place
among the most natural and simple of musical resources. Be this
as it may, the entry of the distant trumpet must inevitably stop
the development; and it becomes interesting to notice that, in
Leonore, No. 3, Beethoven's advance upon his point of view in
Leonore, No. 2, is shown by the fact that in No. 3 he does recognize
that this is no occasion for logical development of his main theme,
but rather for something new that justifies the intervention of
his musical *deus ex machina*. I have already dealt with Grove's
absurd suggestion that the melody which accompanies Leonore's
'*Ach! Du bist gerettet!*' has any connexion with the main theme,
but eventually it leads to the main theme in a key which has
hitherto been crowded out of the Overture, a key which proves
to be the home dominant, in which we have the main theme in
a heavenly dialogue between the flute and bassoon. Thence,
however, we must find our way to our real home tonic; and now
comes that highest and most difficult exercise of Beethoven's
formal power, a slow crescendo with no themes at all. Beethoven
would have been quite bold enough to delight us with Haydn's
practical joke of a false return early in his development, if the
opportunity for such refinements had not been ousted by larger
and more complex matters; but he is capable of the kindred device
of arousing expectation of a return and deferring it. The most
glorious illustration of this is in the fourth of the movements I
cite for comparison, the first movement of the F major Quartet,
op. 59, no. 1. The development has begun with a feint of repeating the exposition. (The whole question of repeats is an interesting
and difficult matter, dependent on the fact that in the sonata forms
we, so to speak, catch melody in the act of breaking up into drama.)

The exposition, with its immensely broad first group and its comparatively terse second group, has prepared us to expect a development on a large scale. But Beethoven has proceeded on broad Mozartean lines, and has hardly transcended them to the extent of introducing a second topic, when he alights upon a chord of the home dominant and proceeds to rouse in us a definite expectation of a return to the tonic. Slowly the harmony moves through the tonic minor, and thence into darker keys, with something of the dignity of an express train that has slowed down in the approach to the junction at which the passenger was expecting to change, until the passenger realizes that he is not in the slip-carriage and that the train is quietly and inexorably passing through. Beethoven reaches the key of ♭VI—not that it matters now to us where we are—and is using his neat little cadence-group to close therein. But the close in diverted into another key, and a new line of development starts off with a double fugue. This, like all fugue passages introduced into sonata developments, takes up considerable room. Eventually it reaches a climax on what is so evidently an enhanced home dominant that we cannot now fail to believe in the signs of a return. In this avenue of approach to our home, the discussion that follows does not seem at first to be more than will pass the time necessary for walking down the avenue; but again we find ourselves turning round a corner and losing sight of our destination. This détour is just long enough to have its own dramatic value, and now, for the last time, we are safely on the home dominant, the violin is climbing upwards, and the rhythm is ready to impinge upon our main theme.

And then it leads to the wrong theme. We are in the right key, but the theme is the short transition figure which originally followed the main theme, and which at the moment had led nowhere. This time, however, it does at last lead very grandly to the main theme. Then, as in the 'Eroica' Symphony, the recapitulation is diversified by further surprises, so we may as well now consider the nature of recapitulations.

To outward appearance, a recapitulation is that part of a musical design which the composer might leave to a copyist after he has ruled the necessary blank bars; and, as a matter of common sense, any composer who knows that he has come to a point where several pages of recapitulation are necessary will probably rule the blank bars and go on to parts in which there is not so much mere copying to be done. But this does not mean that the recapitulation is the part where the composer's imagination ceases to work. On the contrary, no composer has even begun to use his imagination, or, properly speaking, to compose at all, unless he has formed the habit, first, of thinking of every part of his design as of something which either does or does not recur, and secondly, of imagining, as something interesting, the effect which recurrence can be made to produce. An exact recapitulation demands quite as accurate an imagination as a recapitulation varied by ornaments or digressions. Mozart left a large number of unfinished compositions, which are the most tantalizing fragments in the world, because they almost always represent problems which caused him to stop to think. If he afterwards solved any of them in some other work, we may have a faint chance of identifying the problem, though the finished work will have nothing but generalities of design to connect it with the unfinished. Thus, I am able to see that he took two shots at his Clarinet Quintet, and I am very glad that the first shot failed. Several of Mozart's fragments give us a whole composition, and there was a certain Abbé Stadler who showed great skill in finishing them, but the curious thing is that, while Stadler pulls off a plausible Mozart development, he invariably breaks down in the recapitulation.

The same thing is the case with Wilhelmj's completion of an interesting unfinished first movement of a Violin Concerto in C by Beethoven. Wilhelmj's development is not bad, but his recapitulation is entirely wrong. He does not know what ought to be recapitulated in a classical concerto, and he does not know how Beethoven handled such things. It would be unreasonable to demand the genius of Beethoven for a task in conjectural scholarship, and any *a priori* argument would condemn itself which should lay down that Beethoven could not have made an unexpected stroke of genius at any point in his design; but no account of the function of recapitulation in music can possibly be correct which does not recognize that in every recapitulation the imaginative composer knows exactly how his material will be affected by the fact that it has been heard in the exposition. Sonata recapitulations are not mere repetitions: they produce an effect of symmetrical composition, in that, the exposition having consisted of two groups, one in the home tonic and the other in a different key, the recapitulation gives the second group in the home tonic, and thus secures some effect of finality even if there is no coda. Usually, the first group, as well as the second, is recapitulated in the home tonic. This does not normally produce more bulk of home tonic than is necessary to secure a proper balance of key. It obviously makes some difference to the first crucial point of the action; for the transition passage, which we have seen to be a matter needing considerable formal draughtsmanship and dramatic import, must avoid leading to the original foreign key. However, if the transition consists of the old Italian practical joke of pausing on the home dominant and then treating it as a key, this point in the recapitulation will present itself in a new light automatically—that is to say, the old practical joke will be ignored, and the second group will treat the home dominant merely as a home dominant and will follow in the tonic. Once, in quite a late work, the *Namensfeier* Overture, op. 115, Beethoven amused himself and us by doing what had never occurred to any earlier composer, and substituting tonic chords for the formal dominant chords. This is as naïvely witty as the frightened animal in *Winnie the Pooh* who says 'Not at home' to the unrecognized caller, and, when asked: 'But isn't that Piglet's voice?', replies 'It isn't meant to be'.

Such are the extreme cases, the irreducible minima of change in a recapitulation. As a rule, there will be more vital differences. They will naturally tend to concern the first group rather than the second, for we made our first acquaintance with the second group abroad, and when it comes to live with us at home, we may find more satisfaction in its presence than need for variety; but, even so, the music-lover will make far greater progress with his understanding of Beethoven if, instead of regarding the recapitulation as repetition, he keeps his mind alert for fine shades of difference. He will still enjoy all the relaxation that recapitulation can give him, and in the fine details he will get something like that increased feeling of solidity which the observer of a picture obtains when he sees it with one eye, and therefore loses the obvious difference between its flatness and its three-dimensional surroundings. The one-eyed view of the picture does, by an opposite method, what the stereoscope does for the pair of nearly identical pictures that we put into it. The recapitulation makes us see with both eyes what in the exposition we saw with one. Every change in a well-designed recapitulation has that effect, whether it be an enormous and dramatic digression, like the wide modulations imposed upon the first group of the Sonata, op. 106, or the astonishing subtleties which Mozart can compress into a single bar. In the most conventional of all Beethoven's works, the B flat major Sonata, op. 22, the first group is a *locus classicus* for masterful perfunctoriness. But now compare bars 138/139–140 with the corresponding point at bar 11. The extra bars of dialogue have now answered the opening theme in a way which gives the transition that follows all the effect of a solid counterstatement. Again, in the first movement of opus 2, no. 2, the recapitulation omits the counterstatement, bars 21/31, but not until it has developed the dominant close of bars 17/18 into a solid process that gives us the only touch of subdominant in the whole movement.

But the highest power of Beethoven's imagination is shown at points where an exact recapitulation would be ineffective. In the first movement of the F minor Quartet, op. 95, the second group (being in D flat (♭VI)) twice explodes savagely in its flat supertonic. The whole movement is a marvel of terseness, and contrives to pack a large symphonic tragedy into five minutes. The development is a short process of Mozartean straightforwardness and Beethovenish violence, and it leads punctually to a recapitulation in which the first group is represented merely by the moment at which it executed the transition; and here it has the audacity to execute the original transition to the original complementary key (♭VI). After four bars in this key, the second group quietly swings round to the tonic major; but now comes the evidence of Beethoven's imagination at its highest power. Only two other masters could have been trusted to see the right thing here—viz. Schubert and Brahms. Anybody else would have exactly transcribed the fierce outbreaks upon ♭II; but the colour value of ♭II has gone. It is hardly distinguishable from ♭VI. Beethoven substitutes the ordinary supertonic, and does not even sophisticate it by making it major. The glare of common daylight is the one thing that can inspire terror at this juncture.

Nothing is more dangerous to a composer who uses classical forms than the notion that recapitulations need altering merely for the sake of variety. The chief danger is lest what has been proved unnecessary on recurrence should never have proved its necessity in the first instance. Moreover, our text-book notions of form urgently need correcting by an intensive study of the later works of Haydn, in which the very notion of recapitulation is often almost out of place. In finales, Haydn's forms are more regular, mainly because, as we shall see, it is the natural tendency of finales to be comparatively sectional and looser in texture. It seems a platitude to say that whatever happens in a recapitulation, whether in the way of exactness or of freedom, must depend upon the materials to be recapitulated, upon the style of the exposition, upon the events of the development, and upon the possibilities of a coda. A coda was defined by the famous comic singer John Parry as 'a few bars added to the end by way of conclusion', and was illustrated by a gridiron tied to a dog's tail. A real coda is no such optional feature. It is as essential as a peroration, and, in fact, Haydn's codas are perorations; but most people do not realize their existence, because they take the place which Mozart occupies by a regular recapitulation. And Haydn has a way of closing his exposition with a very neat cadence-group, which duly appears at the end of the movement. Our compilers of text-books look no farther. They praise or patronize Haydn as a master of placid symmetries, and they do not realize that Beethoven's largest codas are more like Haydn's perorations than like anything else in earlier music. Mozart's codas are few and are seldom large. The symmetry of his forms is so important that they have more to lose than to gain by the addition of any sort of peroration. Here, as in most other matters, the enormous variety and range of Beethoven's

forms are in large measure a result of integrating the resources of
Haydn together with those of Mozart. Before we consider
Beethoven's codas in themselves, we must realize the extent to
which his recapitulations can be affected by his developments.
This is especially evident in his later works, where the tendency
is to give more and more weight to exposition and recapitulation
—to everything, in short, which seems predestined in the form.
This tendency finds a close parallel in the progress of drama. An
unsophisticated love of what is commonly called 'action' may be
satisfied by a drama in which everything happens visibly and
audibly on the stage, including pistol-shots and the pursuit of
motor-bandits. With growing experience, we come to see that
there may be more drama in actions which appear to consist mainly
of talk, that Destiny is the mightiest of all dramatic forces, and
that some of the most powerful of all dramas consist in revealing
to us that most of the action has happened before the curtain
rose at all.

With Beethoven, there is never any difficulty in seeing where
his recapitulation begins, though we may be surprised when we
find ourselves already in the swing of it; but, where we are thus
surprised, we may find it worth while to remark that the recapitulation is continuing a process begun by the development, especially
when the development has been very short in itself. A clear
illustration of this may be found in the first movement of the
A flat Sonata, op. 110. The development consists in making a
long line of delicately varied descending sequence out of the
figure of the main theme. No two steps of this sequence are quite
alike, but the general tendency is to descend. With a Mozart-like
punctuality, the sequence reaches the home tonic. As its material
is the main theme, the only change that now happens is that the
sequence rises. The counterpoint of the bass changes to the
brilliant figure of the transition-theme and, after four bars, is
transferred to the right hand, while the bass continues the main
theme in further steps of rising sequence, and so takes us to the
subdominant, where the second theme of the first group appears
and executes a remote modulation (♭VI). In this key (F flat=
E natural), the second group actually begins, but slips back into
the home tonic by a purposely indefinite chromatic glide, and
there continues for the rest of the movement. It is evident that
such a recapitulation has actually contained more elements of
diversity than the development itself; and the diversity goes far
beyond what I have already described as the fine touches that
substitute stereoscopic vision for one-eyed vision. The principle
I have compared with stereoscopic vision may itself be worked
out on so vast a scale as to amount to development. The stupen-
dous example is in the finale of the E flat Trio, op. 70, no. 2. In

the exposition, three short themes, all on the tonic, are thrown
at us with no further explanation at the moment than antiphonal repetition as between the pianoforte and the strings. The
transition offers no apology for this abruptness, and, though it
broadens out effectively, the broadening is surprising rather than
explanatory.

Now, if there is any device that could make an opening sound
sequential and formal, it would be the device of answering the
first clauses in the supertonic, as at the beginning of Beethoven's First Symphony. When we come to the recapitulation,
this is what happens. The first pair of themes, having returned
in conspiratorial whispers, begins to repeat itself, and modulates
deliberately to the supertonic, there to begin a counterstatement
which also includes the third theme. This is one of the grandest
architectural effects Beethoven ever produced, and it leads to a
unique feature of form. The second group had been in one of
Beethoven's remoter key-relations, the major mediant (III).
Beethoven's usual practice when he uses this remote key is to let
the recapitulation of the second group represent it by its twin-
brother, the major submediant (VI); but only for a few bars.
With or without the expense of an extra repetition of the first
phrase, the group shifts to the home tonic, and so the normal key-
balance is preserved, though the recapitulation has gained a touch
of brilliant colour. Now, in the finale of the E flat Trio, nothing
could be more natural than that this supertonic, which has so
greatly enlarged the design of the first group, should lead to the
major submediant (VI); but what is unusual and unexpected is
that the whole second group is given in that key, and that afterwards there is another complete recapitulation in the home tonic.

The notion still lingers on from Beethoven's own day that his
later treatment of form was subversive. But if any element of
form might be expected to be regarded with impatience by a
subversive composer, it would be the recapitulation, and the study
of Beethoven's later works shows that it is precisely in recapitulations that Beethoven becomes more and more emphatic, often
stating twice what the exposition stated once. His drama approxi-
mates more and more to that state in which the action has all
happened before the rise of the curtain. People who mistake this
for a decrease in dramatic intensity should realize that they have
not yet begun to know what drama means. Far be it from me to
deny that there is a vital distinction between mere philosophic
discussion and genuinely dramatic dialogue, or to deny so obvious
a fact as that fugue-structure spends in something like philosophic
discussion more room than dramatic musical development can
normally afford; but we really must not trust Beethoven so little
as to acquiesce in the childish assumption that he is less aware of

these considerations than our eminent critics, who seriously believe that Beethoven knew less about fugue-writing than the average candidate for a university musical degree.

It is by this time evident that the words 'exposition', 'development', and 'recapitulation' have nothing to lose, and much to gain, by being applied to music in their usual dictionary sense, instead of being treated as special technical terms. Schubert and Dvořák are common objects of severe criticism for their looseness in the handling of large forms. In as far as the criticism deals with breaches of rule, it cannot be expected to show more intelligence than has been shown in the drawing-up of the orthodox rules; and that may be measured by the fact that the orthodox rules are impossible to apply to any composer greater than Hummel or Spohr. If we charge Schubert with too much repetition in a large movement, we have to face the statistical fact that there is far more repetition in any large movement by Beethoven. The only possible charge to bring against Schubert's repetitions is that he repeats what does not bear repetition, whereas Beethoven evidently repeats what has been designed for the purpose. Everything becomes clear as soon as we use the words 'exposition' and 'development' in their ordinary general sense. Schubert and Dvořák are apt to become prematurely discursive in the business of exposition. Their expositions thus already forestall the function of development; and, when the time for development comes, Schubert is apt to build up large lyric structures which, though new, might have been well placed in an exposition, and which can develop only by repetition occupying enormous space. His returns to the main theme and to the home tonic are often worthy of Beethoven, but the recapitulation is usually not less disastrous from being absolutely necessary. There are not many great codas in Schubert's works. Those in the C major Symphony are again gigantic climaxes not unworthy of Beethoven, but, for the most part, a big Schubert movement dies away with explicit signs of exhaustion. All this criticism obviously might be applied to the early works of a dramatist whose power has not yet developed far enough to control his lyric impulses. But when we come to consider the coda, we shall find that the special musical term is a necessity which cannot be satisfied by any such ordinary word as 'peroration'. There is no general principle that compels a movement to have a peroration. It is no defect of Schubert's codas that they so often frankly represent an expiring from exhaustion; and if a movement can end exactly on the last note of an almost unexpanded recapitulation, as in the first movement of Beethoven's Sonata, op. 22, this may be a *tour de force* in punctuality, as when an oarsman's last stroke brings his boat to the landing-stage and enables him to ship sculls, throw the painter to the waterman, and step on shore in the same moment. On the other hand, there is nothing to prevent the coda from being longer than the whole development and recapitulation together, as in the first movement of *Les Adieux*. Apart from the cases where the coda is a separate section in a quicker, or otherwise different, time, with or without some such wonderful modulation as in the Finales of the Trio, op. 97, and the Quartet, op. 127, there is no reason why the coda should not consist of half the movement, as in the Finale of the Eighth Symphony, unless it be an objection that this upsets our terminology. But the present state of musical terminology is simply not worth taking seriously; and, so long as a writer has defined his own terms and uses them consistently, the reader may, with an easy conscience, acquiesce in Humpty Dumpty's policy of letting words mean just what he chooses, so long as he pays them extra wages for extra work.

It is a not unusual characteristic of finales that they make comparatively short work of the business of formal symmetry in order to have leisure to expand in a coda. In such a case, the coda will be typically a peroration, and the musical features of a peroration will easily show their kinship with those of a peroration in words. For instance, topics that were introduced separately will be combined in the same sentence. Sequences that were 'real' in their original statement will become 'tonal'; that is to say, whereas the original sequence consisted of transpositions to a foreign key at each step, the sequence in the peroration will be within the key, and will alter its tones and semitones according to the part of the scale in which it falls. For instance, in the first movement of the 'Waldstein' Sonata, op. 53, compare bars 1–8, which are in real sequence, modulating boldly through the enhanced subdominant, with bars 261–268, where you will find the main theme in the bass in what is essentially tonal sequence, implying a firm position on the home dominant throughout. (The supertonic colouring during the first four-bar limb of the sequence does not destroy the dominant impression: you could sustain a dominant pedal through it without making any difference to the sense.)

The most characteristic feature in Beethoven's larger codas may be called the 'tonic-and-dominant swing', which may pile up, as in the 'Eroica' and Ninth Symphony, to a tremendous climax. The nature of such a climax is not dramatic, but rhetorical. It has no element of suspense. On the contrary, it implies quite literally that all is over except the shouting.

The grandeur of a coda of this type is quite different from the architectural climaxes of Bach, though the paradox of it is that it has the quality of Bach's punctuality. The study of Beethoven's

proportions in these matters has hardly yet begun. Many writers
have discovered that the proportions of classical sonata movements
fall into golden sections: that is to say, where it is possible
to trace a division into two unequal parts, the ratio of the less to
the greater will be the same as that of the greater to the sum.
There are two difficulties about applying this fascinating theory
to music, even where it works (and doubtless it sometimes does)
as well in music as in sculpture and architecture. The main
difficulty is that of appreciating time-values as if they were space-
values. We may unload this difficulty on to that patient ass, the
subconscious. A more serious difficulty is that there are so many
possible ways of dividing large musical designs that you could
hardly fail to discover golden sections anywhere and everywhere.
I have no means of proving to the reader that Beethoven's proportions are always right. No two examples are alike. All I can say
is that, while there are some errors, or, rather, unresolved conflicts,
to be found in Beethoven's works, I have studied his proportions
ever since I had any musical memory at all and have always found
that the notion that Beethoven is extravagant or incorrect in this
matter bases itself on the critics' own complete failure to attend
to the matter in hand. The reader cannot be too strongly advised
to dismiss from his mind any idea that a classical orthodoxy in
musical form exists at all. Good teachers of composition simply
do not teach out of a text-book, and the fact by which the self-
styled classical rules stand self-condemned is that they were drawn
up by contemporaries of the great classics; that is to say,
they were drawn up by people who would gladly have persecuted
Haydn, Mozart, and Beethoven as heretics.

One other feature of Beethoven's large codas is important, and
may be taken as a point of departure for considering the most
difficult and dangerous of all classical art-forms, the concerto. In
making a final cadence, the usual antepenultimate chord, itself an
ornament of the penultimate chord, is the 6/4. On this the singer

Ex.20

or the solo player, was already accustomed in and before the time
of Bach and Handel to extemporize a flourish, while the orchestra
first paused for a while on the chord and then waited in silence
while the singer displayed his voice and his breathing-powers.
With self-supporting solo instruments, the cadenza became free
to develop in interesting ways, and while it could legitimately

retain the manner of an extemporization, there was no reason why it should abandon regular rhythm as it does in the passages already cited from Beethoven's early Sonatas, opus 2, no. 3, and the Violoncello Sonata, opus 5, no. 1. The coda of the first movement of the 'Waldstein' Sonata contains a typical short cadenza, which is in strict time except for the pauses which lead to one of Beethoven's most beautiful strokes of genius, the cantabile theme of the second group with its cadence twice interrupted. The notorious octave glissando in the prestissimo coda to the finale is the beginning of another cadenza, which, though without definite theme, is rhythmically unbroken. In the interesting and perhaps unconscious study for the 'Waldstein' Sonata, the G major Sonata, op. 31, no. 1, there is a highly organized quasi-fugal cadenza towards the end of the finale, bar 206 onwards. As befits the style of the work, it fails to keep up its countenance, and relapses into excellent fooling à la Haydn, causing the pretty main theme to dress up its alternate phrases as a solemn adagio, and eventually running away with an uncontrollable attack of giggling. The final presto of the Finale of the C minor Symphony is the outcome of a grand contrapuntal cadenza for the full orchestra.

Apropos of the cadenza, it will now be convenient to consider Beethoven's treatment of concerto form. On the whole, if there is any use in advice about the order in which Beethoven's works should be heard, it is perhaps as well to have found one's way about his sonata forms before trying to understand the concertos. At all events, by far the easiest way to describe classical concerto is to present it in the light of a sonata that has been projected against a symphonic orchestral background. Apart from historic origins, the problem of sharing a large sonata form between a solo player, or solo group, and an orchestra is by no means simple, and its solution by Mozart is by no means conventional, but is one of the highest manifestations of Mozart's intellectual and dramatic power. Beethoven himself did not fully understand the problem in his first three concertos. He solved it correctly in a gigantic exercise, the Triple Concerto, op. 56, which is in this unfortunate position, that the experiment of writing for the new kind of concerto-group led Beethoven to use dry themes in order to concentrate attention on tone-colour, just as Mozart used formulas rather than individual themes when writing for a wind-band. This would not have mattered, but for the fact that enormous length was necessary for the exposition of this material by three solo instruments instead of one. Mozart can be at his best with music in which the themes do not distract attention from the colours, and he can also be at his best in solving an art-problem where he needs plenty of elbow-room; but you will not catch him attempting both these problems at once and compelling himself to handle dry material at extreme length.

In the time of Bach and Handel, concerto form was an enlarged example of the form of a vocal aria. The orchestra justifies its existence by summing up the gist of the matter in a single pregnant paragraph. The voice or the solo instrument treats this matter as the Carthaginian settlers treated the ox-hide which they cut into strips wherewith to stake out the boundaries of their city. At each angle of the city wall, so to speak—that is to say, at each cadence in a related key—the orchestra intervenes with the whole or part of the ritornello. The solo episodes will have a natural tendency to grow, and before the movement concludes with the final ritornello in the home tonic, a considerable climax may be obtained, with or without a cadenza. All this is quite easy to handle so long as the music does not overstep the bounds of rhetoric and enter the Gluck-Haydn-Mozart regions of drama; in other words, so long as your modulations treat the home tonic like a tournament horse which will allow you to get on and off it as if it were a table; but, when you are dealing with a music in which such devices as dominant preparation will cause your home tonic to sink below the horizon, then it is by no means easy for a solo instrument and an orchestra to combine in a serious art-form.

The contrast between the solo and the orchestra is, of course, that between the individual and a crowd. The solo part will naturally consist chiefly of things that the orchestra cannot do nearly so well, and the art-form will to that extent justify the derivation of its name from *concertare*, to strive with. Hence, Prout's unfortunate statement in Grove's *Dictionary* that 'this name is now given to an instrumental composition designed to show the skill of the executant'. Prout is the victim, not the originator, of this notion, which has vulgarized the whole orthodox notion of one of the sublimest of art-forms. Naturally, there is an immensely greater number of vulgar concertos than of sublime ones. When a composer produces a new symphony, we all expect nowadays that it will be something serious, even if the composer happens to be a great player; but when a composer produces a new concerto, not only is he usually expected to produce something vulgar, but, if he should produce a work on classical lines, he will be told, as Brahms was told, that he is only producing a symphony with obbligato for pianoforte or violin, and that the solo part is quite inaudible. Nobody with a sense of style has the slightest doubt that Beethoven's three greatest concertos, the G major, op. 58, and E flat, op. 73, for pianoforte, and the Violin Concerto, op. 61, are among his grandest works. Every element in them is at its highest power. The orchestra is not only symphonic, but is enabled, by the very necessity of accompanying the solo lightly, to produce ethereal orchestral effects that are in quite a different category from anything in the symphonies. On the other hand, the solo part develops the technique of its instrument with a freedom and brilliance for which Beethoven has no leisure in sonatas and chamber music. Nowadays, the difficulty of understanding these works is of two kinds. First, there are very few of them, even if we add, as the culmination of Beethoven's first style, the C minor Concerto. Secondly, the very naïve listener enjoys the solo part as fireworks and misses all other values. In virtue of his enjoyment of the fireworks, however, he is in better case than the listener with a conscientious objection to popular elements, for to such a listener the classical concerto is a book sealed with seven seals. The only composer who has produced a large number of concertos in the highest classical form is Mozart, of whom at least sixteen concertos are on the level of his great chamber music and his last symphonies. Brahms rediscovered the true form or forms, and produced four monumental works, radically different from each other, as are Beethoven's masterpieces. The masters between Beethoven and Brahms had not the slightest idea of the question at issue. Mendelssohn, who is popularly supposed to work on classical lines, produced quite a new thing in his beautiful Violin Concerto and his two perfunctory Pianoforte Concertos: a good and effective thing as far as it goes, but definitely of a lighter order of music. Space forbids me to go into further details, but we shall be prepared to understand Beethoven's concertos correctly if we simply realize that the function of the orchestra is not unlike that of the chorus in Greek drama.

In the first movement of a concerto, the orchestra gives out a large procession of themes—in other words, the Bach-Handel aria ritornello has expanded into quite a long story; but we must not make the mistake which Beethoven himself actually made, and corrected in the making, in the first tutti of his C minor Concerto. This procession of themes is not a sonata exposition. In the C minor Concerto, Beethoven actually thought that it was, and established his second group in its complementary key by means of a long passage of dominant preparation which threw the tonic completely below the horizon. Having got thus far, it suddenly seems to occur to Beethoven that there is no reason why this work should not be a symphony. The pianoforte is there in the background without the slightest motive for intervening. The mischief being already done, the orchestra calmly explains it away by sliding round to the home tonic, in which key it adds a few more cadential themes and comes to a very complete close. Then the pianoforte enters, and for some time

can do nothing but turn the whole symphonic statement into the
sonata exposition which it already is, hardly even daring to expand
the passages of dominant preparation, which was already long
enough in the opening tutti. After this, all is well. The pianoforte can release itself from paraphrasing the opening tutti
and can expand and expatiate as a solo part should. In Beethoven's
first two Concertos, C major, op. 15, and B flat, op. 19, he had
not made his opening tutti so dangerously like a symphonic
opening; but he had produced a mass of delightful discursiveness
as if the orchestra were extemporizing. This, of course, is simply
making the orchestra do the pianoforte's business, and while it
does not, like a symphonic opening, positively contradict the
prospect of the entry of a solo, it does nothing to make it expected.
In the G major Concerto, Beethoven allows the pianoforte to
play the first five bars, and in the E flat Concerto there is a
cadenza-like introduction, in which key-chords from the full
orchestra are answered with arpeggios and declamation *senza
tempo* by the pianoforte. In both cases, the orchestra proceeds
with a ritornello on the largest possible scale: in spite of which,
our standard work of reference tells us that in these works Beethoven abolished the opening tutti. In the Violin Concerto, the
opening tutti is again on the largest possible scale, and so is that
of the Triple Concerto, an unlucky work which repays sym-
pathetic study. What is common to all these great tuttis is that
quality, recaptured by Beethoven and Brahms from Mozart, by
which the procession of themes arouses the expectation that some
master is coming whose words will hold us spellbound. What
the solo instrument does, when it arrives, is to produce a symphonic sonata-form, on the largest scale, on the materials of the
tutti plus materials of its own. During the tutti, there is no means
of knowing which of the themes will belong to the first or which
to the second group, or even of knowing which of them will be
used by the solo part at all. First and second group, and other
elements of sonata form, do not, in fact, come into existence until
the solo instrument creates them. In the G major Concerto, the
second group, when it arrives, is introduced by an entirely new
orchestral theme. In the Triple Concerto, the transition is
effected by a new orchestral theme, which produces two dramatic
surprises by entering in unexpectedly remote keys, first at the
beginning of the development, and secondly at the beginning of
the coda.

In these circumstances, it is not very easy to say what innova-
tions Beethoven produced in concerto form. By far the most
important and difficult problem is the relation between the tutti
and the solo—in fact, the construction of the opening tutti itself;
and, as no two opening tuttis of Mozart, Beethoven, and Brahms

are on anything like the same plan, either in themselves or in
their relation to the solo instrument, it is unprofitable to generalize.
Two things Beethoven did unquestionably develop. First, acting
on a hint only twice given by Mozart, he made his solo instrument
enter, as in the Violin Concerto, with a long preludial passage.
Secondly—and this is a stroke which he already achieved with
great power in the C minor Concerto—Beethoven contrives that
when the orchestra re-enters after the exposition, while recapitulating a more or less large portion of the opening tutti, it shall
shift in its uninterrupted course to a new key; so that the development has already obtained great impetus before it sets out on
lines of its own. The development itself tends to become episodic.
This is a natural consequence of the contrast between solo and
orchestra. An ordinary symphonic development would tend either
to suppress the orchestra, to overwhelm the solo, or to fall into
crudely contrasted sections. It is this danger of sectionality that
has produced the extraordinary devices of Mozart's and Beethoven's
concerto ritornellos, and these devices would never have come
into being from meaner motives than that of realizing in the
concerto style the sublime power of the individual over the crowd.
Slow movements and finales can do with simpler and more
sectional forms, and so in them the problem of the concerto had
no special difficulty. The minuet or scherzo, on the other hand,
is too sectional for concerto treatment until it has grown to the
gigantic dimensions of the second movement of Brahms's B flat
Pianoforte Concerto. Accordingly, there are no concertos by
Mozart or Beethoven in more than three movements.

THE RONDO AND OTHER SECTIONAL
FORMS

THE type of form shown in the first movements of sonatas contains all the elements of Beethoven's art in its highest state of organization. When we have grasped its principles clearly, most of the other art-forms explain themselves as simplifications of what we have already learnt. In taking advantage of this, we must beware lest it lead us into the common error of estimating our musical values simply by counting up their obvious intellectual assets. We have already seen how foolish this is with passages taken out of their context. It is not less foolish, and it is a much more likely error, in the case of whole movements and whole art-forms.

The commonest form of this error is that which invariably criticizes a small, or light-hearted, finale as the weak point of a work. We need not suppose that Beethoven is infallible. He often changed his mind in the earlier stages of a composition, and in two important instances he wrote a new finale, transferring the original brilliant finale of the Violin Sonata, op. 30, no. 1, to the 'Kreutzer' Sonata, partly because it was too brilliant for the earlier work, and partly because he had arranged for a public performance of the 'Kreutzer' Sonata and had no time to write any other finale. The first movement of the 'Kreutzer' Sonata is immeasurably finer than the rest of the work, but the criticism that despises the rest of the work is based on the assumption that, in works that proceed in time, the best should be reserved for the end. And this is simply not true. In the first place, as the eminent painter asked of the brainless athlete who said he could not keep fit on less than so many hours' exercise a day, 'Fit for what?'—best for what? That finale is best which is the most refreshing after what has gone before; and it is an invariable rule with finales that their texture is in some way less concentrated than that of first movements. This becomes very obvious when the finale is in the form of a first movement. Its statements will be content to lie side by side without amplification, and its transitions will seldom be elaborate affairs.

The case of a slow movement in first-movement form is interesting in another way. Slowness, as has already been observed, must mean bigness if it means anything, and the difficulty of working out a slow movement in sonata form is that, even with the tersest of procedures, its dimensions become enormous; but it has not the kind of urgency that makes the finale perfunctory in its transitions. On the contrary, nothing can be grander and more suited to a slow movement than that the transition from the first to the second group shall be of full classical breadth, provided that the composer understands the matter from the point of view of the listener, and realizes that three or four bars of slow common time are as expensive a matter in his musical planning as half an acre in the City of London to a speculative builder.

Very grand slow movements can be constructed in a sonata form that omits the development. The omission of the development reduces the bigness of the total impression far less than any perfunctoriness in the transition or shortness in the recapitulation. Mozart produced slow movements of this kind without development; apart from the two great early tragic slow movements of the Sonata, op. 10, no. 3, and the Quartet, op. 18, no. 1, Beethoven's style had matured to that of his second period before he could transcend Mozart in such designs. But Mozart also designed great slow movements with developments. A few of these, such as that in the D major Quintet, are quite slow, but more usually Mozart solves the problem of first-movement form in slow movements by making the tempo a flowing andante, in which case he can afford to direct that the exposition be repeated, and even the development and recapitulation. Beethoven produced several delightful slow movements on these lines, the latest being that of the A minor Violin Sonata, op. 23, unless we choose to say that the Scherzo of the E flat Sonata, op. 31, no. 3, which is marked *allegretto vivace*, is a slow movement, on the grounds that by position it cannot possibly be anything else, though it is very much faster than the following minuet and trio.

It is of some importance to be able to recognize where a slow movement is in full sonata form, because this is one of the things that can be done by ear, and must not be entrusted to the eye. The commonest mistake which the merely optical analyst makes is that of counting the bars and supposing that seven or eight of them cannot be enough to constitute a development. The listener need make no such mistake. The single dominant chord that marks off a bar in the middle of the slow movement of opus 10, no. 1, obviously does not amount to a development. Neither do the four or five bars—five, if you count the overlap with the previous theme—in the middle of the slow movement of opus 31, no. 2, constitute a development. The ear could tell us, without counting the ticking of a seconds-hand, that nothing has happened except a passage of preparation on the home dominant. The eight bars in the same position in the middle of the slow movement of the D major Trio, op. 70, no. 1, are scarcely longer by the ticking of the seconds hand, but there are three modulations in the first three bars, a complete change of topic in the next four, and the last bar is equivalent to a full-sized preparation for the home tonic. More has happened here than in the quite orthodox, though short, development of the finale, which occupies about a couple of pages. In the largest of all Beethoven's slow movements, that of the Sonata, op. 106, the development again looks short on paper, but to the ear it is one of the longest and most labyrinthine sequences in all sonata-music. Beethoven produced not less than twenty movements in full sonata form, besides two or three cases, such as in the Septet and the C minor Concerto, where the recapitulation, though not the development, has been short-circuited, and six or seven in which the development has been omitted. Apart from the listener's capacity to recognize development when he hears it, there is no interest in classifying border-line cases. But it does concern the listener to understand how border-line cases can arise. They arise from the fact that a slow movement being naturally the most lyric part of a sonata, its themes are likely to have the quality of a rondo theme.

Now, according to the old misleading classification of forms as binary and ternary, the rondo is a product of ternary form. The so-called 'binary' form has, as we have seen, developed by enormous expansion. Starting from a melody which may be as compact as 'Barbara Allen', it grows first into the dance-forms of Bach's suites, which may swell out to the giant-gooseberry experience of a Boccherini 'cello sonata, and then passes, as we have seen, into the state in which single melody is altogether transcended and the tremendous dramatic power of Beethoven's sonata form becomes possible. Thus expansion is the only way in which the so-called 'binary' form is developed. The ternary form, on the other hand, has two lines of development: the first, by expansion. This may be the mere juxtaposition of two complete objects made into three by a da capo of the first, as in the case of the minuet and trio, or scherzo and trio; or it may be the larger types of ABA form, in which B, though a central episode, may become quite a venturesome affair with a dramatic interest, culminating in the return to A. If there is a coda that alludes to the adventures of B, we have an important art-form, of which Beethoven's *locus classicus* is the Allegretto which does duty for slow movement in the F minor Quartet, op. 95; but the ternary form can develop on quite different lines: viz. by multiplication, without enlarging its elements at all. Instead of ABA, we may have AB AC AD, etc.; and if A is a single epigrammatic strain, we get the *rondeau en couplets* of Couperin and Bach, which in the *chansons* of Orlando di Lasso is the automatic result of his setting the *rondeaux* of Ronsard and other French poets.

Now, suppose that the rondo has passed beyond the stage of the Bach-Couperin *rondeau en couplets*, and that the episodes, instead of being *couplets*, are more or less like the second groups of sonata-form movements; you will soon see that a border-line case is very likely to occur; for, if the change of key to the first episode has been effected by a serious effort of musical draughts-manship, like the transition to a second group, it is evident that the composer is losing his opportunities if, in the penultimate stages of the movement, he does not recapitulate this episode in the home tonic. His second episode is, of course, often another lyric melody in another key; but there is nothing to prevent it from leading to adventurous developments, or consisting wholly of a line of developments of previous material. Then, if, after the second return of the rondo theme, the first episode is recapi-tulated in the tonic, there is only one point at which the rondo differs from sonata form, and that is in the immediate return of the first theme in the tonic after the exposition. But even this may be a distinction without a difference, for, when a sonata movement repeats its exposition, it produces for the moment precisely the effect of a rondo return, and we only gradually discover that we are listening to a mere repetition. Moreover, when the composer has given up the idea of repeating his exposi-tion, he often begins his development by a return to the opening as in opus 59, no. 1; and if the opening is tunelike, then the distinction between sonata form and rondo form seems to have broken down altogether. In the case of the F minor Quartet, op. 95, I frankly do not know, and do not care, what you call the finale. Its theme is midway in style between a rondo theme and a first-movement theme. It returns immediately after an episode, or second group, in the dominant, but is represented only by four bars, after which its figures continue in a very short development. But though there are, thus, border-line cases, there is usually surprisingly little difficulty in recognizing when one is listening to a movement in rondo style. In spite of the great melodic breadth of the openings of opus 59, no. 1, and opus 97, nobody can possibly suppose that the way in which those immense themes expand is the way in which a tune behaves when its purport is to return in its integrity as often as possible—in short, to behave like a tune, not like a piece of dramatic business.

Beethoven has none of the superior modern teacher's contempt for rondo form and style. He will not write a first movement in rondo form, but considerably more than half of his one hundred and one acknowledged works in sonata form have rondo finales, and his power of compression in slow movements is such that he several times achieves a full-sized rondo, in three cases a sonata-form rondo, in an adagio or an andante. Poor Schubert, as usual, gets blamed for being unable to resist the temptation to repeat too much, and in the case of Schubert's rondos, even more than in the case of his first movements, the real difficulty is that, being

discursive at the wrong points, his rondos cannot bear the irreducible amount of repetition on which they must live. With
Beethoven, whatever may be inherent in the art-forms that he
takes over from his predecessors, he develops that character to
its fullest extent. The characteristic of a rondo has been well
described by Parry as 'the frequent and desirable return of a
melody of great beauty'. People have been known to complain
that the rondo of opus 90 repeats itself too much. They should
join company with the sea-captain who took up a copy of *Gulliver's
Travels* and, after reading several chapters, flung it down, ex-
claiming: 'I don't believe a word of it.' Tastes may differ about
the desirability of hearing the beautiful melody of the rondo of
opus 90 three times unvaried in full, with its own self-repetitions,
and a fourth time as a duet between treble and bass, plus a compressed final version in the coda, making ten times in all for the
first clause. But when this rondo is cited as an unusually long
movement, taste has nothing to do with the matter. It so happens
that the whole thing is compressed into six and a half minutes.
Beethoven has written some of the longest movements that have
ever been held together in perfect form. But no other composer
is a match for him in power of compression; nor, until Wagner
changed the whole time-scale of music, has anybody approached
Beethoven in power of expansion. The very nature of Wagner's
achievement prevents him from approaching Beethoven in the
power of conveying an impression of vastness in a short time.
Beethoven's rondos show this with quite as much power as his
first movements: there is not room in the art of music for a greater
sense of space than the developments of the second episodes in
the rondos of the 'Waldstein' Sonata and the E flat Concerto.

In Beethoven's earlier works, we find another kind of rondo,
more nearly related to the old *rondeau en couplets*. Its characteristics are: first, that its theme is a single strain, with or without
a couple of echoing tags; secondly, that its episodes at first tend
to be definitely sectional, though, later on, the movement may
become more highly organized; and thirdly, that there is probably
an episode, or even more than one episode, in the home tonic
at the end, so as to provide a large and expanding coda. There
is also nothing to prevent the influence of sonata form on such
a rondo, by making the first episode recur later on in the home
tonic. This is very clearly seen in the finale of op. 13, the *Sonata
Pathétique*. This kind of rondo, which is more or less typical of
Haydn, Beethoven also uses in some of his early slow movements,
opus 2, no. 2, and the Violin Sonata, op. 30, no. 1. In these
cases Beethoven is fond of the leisurely effect of a sort of epilogue-
episode in the home tonic, a device expensive of space in a
slow tempo, but admirably suited to a mood of relaxation. The

slow movement of the 'Pastoral' Symphony is in full-sized sonata form with a very spacious development and full recapitulation. The famous passage representing the cuckoo, the nightingale, and the quail occupies far less space in the coda, and is far more closely fitted into the phrasing of the main themes, than any of these earlier final episodes. This fact ought to dispose of the nonsense that has been written both in praise and blame of Beethoven for departing from absolute music in those works in which he happens to mention an external object as a source of his inspiration.

In a slow tempo, it is even more of a *tour de force* to work out a sonata-form rondo than a first movement; yet Beethoven already achieved this triumphantly in the slow movement of the Trio, op. 1, no. 1; and the slow movement of the Fourth Symphony is a magnificent example. For the rest, the listener should not worry about the names of the forms, and still less about the classification of border-line cases. Occasionally, he may encounter a paradox, such as the theme of the rondo of opus 10, no. 3, which is obviously not a tune, though events show it to be the theme of a rondo; but there is no danger of mistaking this paradox for anything but what it is. If it is not a tune, it is certainly an epigram, and it is fulfilling its obvious destiny in developing into a rondo structure instead of an example of first-movement form. On the other hand, there is no reason why a finale that begins with a typical rondo theme should not turn out, like the finale of the Eighth Symphony, to be in first-movement form—that is to say, to reduce to a mere starting-point of development the return to the theme after the first episode. We need no application to know more about such matters than Mozart, who would cheerfully call a theme a rondo, even though it has divided itself into the two repeated sections of a sonata movement. All that concerns the listener is what he can hear from moment to moment and all the time. What he hears in a movement in rondo style is that the opening theme has rounded itself off either like an epigram or like a complete lyric stanza. In other words, the distinction is that which we drew between the so-called 'binary' and 'ternary' forms—between a form in which the first member is incomplete and that in which it is complete.

VARIATIONS

TWO other art-forms remain for consideration: variations and fugue.

Bad variations are even commoner, because much easier to write, than bad concertos, and the chief danger in criticizing Beethoven's variations arises from the fact that the intellectually interesting type of variation, which Beethoven developed farther than any other composer before or since, is much less often appropriate to his larger designs than the simplest type of embroidery variation, which no technical analysis can distinguish from the vulgarest effusions of salon music. Let us, therefore, consider the more interesting kinds of variations first. They all exist as independent works, for it is only in independent works that the composer is free to treat his variation theme in ways that disguise the melody beyond recognition. In the sonata style, we recognize events by identifying themes in their melodic aspect, and to expect us to abandon this habit of mind is like expecting us to enjoy a drama in which all the characters are liable to disguise themselves and to change their names; but in a theme for variations the melody is but one aspect of the theme, and the kind of theme that will bear highly intellectual variations may or may not be in keeping with sonata style at all. Beethoven has given us an extremely interesting case of a variation theme which he first developed as an independent work and later worked out, in a form compounded of variations and other elements, as the finale of the 'Eroica' Symphony. The style and treatment of the variations in the 'Eroica' Symphony are far more gorgeous than that of the Pianoforte Variations, op. 35, but the Pianoforte Variations contain many transformations of the theme that would be entirely unrecognizable as such if they occurred in the Symphony.

My own classification of composers of variations is into those who show that they know their theme and those who show that they do not. The wording of this definition is important. It has been misquoted as 'those who remember their theme and those who forget it', but the fact is that Mendelssohn, whom I am sorry to be once more treating as an Aunt Sally, simply did not know his own theme when he wrote the *Variations Sérieuses*. It has a magnificent structure, and, if he had recognized that, he could have got away from the melody, while remaining perfectly faithful to the form. As it was, he could neither get away from it nor stick to it. The only variations which have any solidity are those in which he is content with mere embroidery.

Throughout this discussion, I have always insisted that the listener must believe in nothing that does not reach his ear, and I am now going to test this rule in a paradoxical way. Recent writers have shown that the classical doctrine of variation form, recovered with extraordinary pains and thoroughness by Brahms, and taught with the utmost clearness to his pupils by Parry, has fallen again into oblivion. We are told that, while Bach's 'Goldberg' Variations are magnificent music, only an optimist would call them variations; and Brahms's Variations on a theme of Handel are praised because in them we can still detect the melody. Now the demonstrably classical facts are that both Bach's 'Goldberg' Variations and Beethoven's Thirty-three Variations on a waltz by Diabelli, with two exceptions in the 'Diabelli' Variations, are absolutely strict: quite as strict as the strictest fugue that was ever written to demonstrate the principles of its form to students. (Here I must interpolate that the so-called classical rules of fugue are the most entirely fictitious rules in the whole history of academic bluff, and that I shall take no notice of them whatever in dealing with Beethoven's fugues.)

The listener who wishes to understand Beethoven's variations had better begin at once by relieving his conscience of all responsibility for tracing the melody. Moreover, he need not worry about his capacity to trace the harmony. Nor, indeed, is there any single musical category which will suffice as the basis of the 'Diabelli' Variations. Nothing short of the whole theme will answer the purpose. Each variation may single out one or more aspects of this whole, and the listener may enjoy all resemblances that attract his attention. All further effort on his part is mistaken, and if there seems to be no definable resemblance between the variation and the theme, the listener is entitled to welcome the variety as a complete change. One thing, however, is present in all genuine classical variations, and that is the momentum set up by the recurring period of the theme as a whole. To interpolate a digression, or to alter the phrase-lengths of a variation, is to incur a risk which the great masters of classical variation-form hardly ever venture. A great set of variations is not, as so many people are apt to guess on *a priori* grounds, a patchwork; nor is it a set of riddles. It is a kind of music with the enormous momentum of something that revolves on its axis or moves in an orbit. The highest problem in the art of variation-making is to stop this momentum. In the 'Goldberg' Variations, Bach achieves this by consummate mastery in the grouping of the whole set, so that the simple direction *aria da capo* brings the work to a close as completely satisfactory as if the great Queen herself had returned and made a royal curtsey before the assembly of all her descendants. In the variations at the end of the Sonata, op. 109, Beethoven achieves a similar *tour de force* with the aid of only three bars deferring the close of the last variation; after which he finishes the sonata with a da capo of the theme.

In other works, the problem of bringing a set of variations to a close is one of the most difficult in all art. It is easiest when the set of variations is obviously an independent work, for then the last variation can fly off at a tangent and develop as a fugue, or some other movement with a form of its own. The expression 'flying off at a tangent' is almost literally true, if the independent movement has begun with the whole, or part, of the theme in a recognizable form, for then we are actually moving under the impetus of what I have already described as the orbital, or diurnal, rotation of the theme. On the other hand, this impetus may have been reduced by a variation which takes the theme in a very slow tempo, as in the 'Prometheus' Variations, op. 35, the material of which is afterwards so gloriously used as the finale of the 'Eroica' Symphony. Notice that the slow tempo does not annihilate the diurnal momentum of the theme. The slow variation may be, as in Beethoven's opus 35, in virtue of its tempo, six times as large as its theme, but so long as it keeps its shape, we are throughout conscious of seeing the theme magnified.

The adagio variation, numbered fifteen in the 'Prometheus' set, is very instructive, because it has a coda in which the theme is ingeniously transformed into quite a new rhythm nine bars before the lively fugue which follows as an independent movement. This transformation, which compresses the first part of the theme from eight bars into two, does really, and of set purpose, annihilate the momentum, and tells us that the composition has left the orbit of the theme. Beethoven makes as if to repeat this rhythmic transformation of the theme, but diverts it to a half-close into the dominant of C minor, and thereon arouses anticipation for some new event. The new event is a lively fugue on the first four notes of the bass of the theme. The whole set of variations has really been, not fifteen, as Beethoven says, but nineteen, for the *Introduzione col Basso del Tema* propounded the absolutely bare bass as a theme and adorned it into two-part, three-part, and four-part counterpoint, before the melody, entitled *tema*, arrived. Thus, when Beethoven writes a fugue on the initial figure of this bass, we have no difficulty in understanding the allusion, and in the same way the same introductory procedure of building by counterpoint on the bare bass enables him to design the finale of the 'Eroica' Symphony as a unique compound of variations with fugal and other episodes in a wide range of key.

But the device that gives full power and finality to Beethoven's variation codas consists in this: that, after he has effectively flown off at a tangent and enjoyed his freedom, the old diurnal spin returns in more effective shape than a mere da capo of the theme, and we have one or more supplementary variations and fragments of variations, each of which runs into the next instead of coming to a formal close. In fact, the spin behaves very much like that of a teetotum before it comes to a stop. In the 'Prometheus' Variations and in the 'Eroica' Finale, the return to the diurnal rotation is the more effective inasmuch as the theme is at half tempo. In the 'Eroica' Finale this poco andante sets up its own majestic momentum and expands in some of the deepest and most moving passages in the Symphony.

In the greatest of all variation works, the Thirty-three Variations on a waltz of Diabelli, there are no less than three variations in a slow tempo, Variations 29, 30, 31; and the free movement entitled Variation 32 is a fugue suggested by a mere tag of Diabelli's absurd theme. It is in a foreign key ($\flat$III), and the return to the home tonic is worked by one of the most mysterious and marvellous of Beethoven's modulations. The device of changing one chord into another is often used by Beethoven as the most unmistakable of all demonstrations of key-relation. Here it conceals the key-relation with still more consummate art. Then the theme returns in a final variation as a very slow and most ethereal minuet; after which, there is a die-away coda with an appropriate touch of subdominant; but even then, sixteen bars before the end, you will find the music beginning to rotate once more in the diurnal spin of Diabelli's theme, with its long lines of tonic and dominant, followed by its shorter lines of sequence. Diabelli's theme has often been cited as a proof that Beethoven could make the most enormous works out of nothing. This is not true. He could not have made an enormous set of variations out of the sublime themes which he treats in variation form in his sonata works. Diabelli's theme is as prosaic as the hard-shell business-man who wrote it, but it does mean business, and a stronger structure has never been realized in reinforced concrete. It is a theme which sets the composer free to build recognizable variations in every conceivable way. It was sent by Diabelli to fifty-one eminent musicians living in Austria, and Diabelli's purpose was to collect from each musician a variation and to publish the whole fifty-one for the benefit of the widows and orphans in the late wars. Beethoven was about to begin on the Ninth Symphony, and his first impulse was doubtless to advise Diabelli with Beethovenish precision to go Elsewhere. Instead of which, after keeping Diabelli on tenterhooks for a considerable time, he sent a contribution which had to be published in a separate volume. I have seen the volume containing the other fifty contributions. These range from one Assmayer to a person whose name I have forgotten, but it begins with Z and continues with several other consonants. One of the

variations is among the earliest extant works of Liszt, who was
at that time eleven. Another is by Schubert, and Schubert at
his best. A third is by S.K.H.R., His Imperial Highness the
Archduke Rudolph, who vindicates his musicianship by writing
a fugue. I will not undertake to pass an examination in any of
these variations except Schubert's, but the glance I have taken
at the volume is quite enough to show that most of the composers,
from the excellent Assmayer to the gentleman with a name like
a sneeze, found Diabelli's theme a surprisingly plastic object. I
quote the first half in full to show its form. T stands for tonic
and D for dominant.

Ex. 21

It will be seen that the short sequential lines are placed between
a couple of long lines and what might be called a prize last line
in a scheme closely resembling that of a limerick. Now it is
obviously legitimate to substitute one tonic and dominant form
for another as long as they both fill up the same space. For
instance, the formal TTTD, DDDT (as at the beginning of the
finale of the D minor Sonata, op. 31, no. 2) is a legitimate altera-
tion for Diabelli's four tonics and four dominants. Then again,
Diabelli's melody (and why not call it melody when railway
companies classify typewriters as musical instruments?) begins
with a twiddle around the tonic, and repeats the twiddle a step
higher over the dominant. Accordingly it is quite natural, and
productive of great variety, to translate the first eight bars from

a tonic and dominant antithesis to a tonic and supertonic sequence (Var. 8); and, if supertonic, why not flat supertonic (Var. 30)? Again, the bass is as recognizable a melody as the treble. In fact, poor Leporello sang it at the beginning of *Don Giovanni*, when the curtain rose upon his unwilling sentry-go during his master's most wicked escapade (Variation 22, *Alla 'Notte e giorno faticar' di Mozart*). Very rarely does Beethoven take liberties with the actual size of the theme. In two variations, he omits a bar, almost certainly by inadvertence, which is not unlikely, considering the desperate hurry in which this most wonderful of variation-works was written. In the Mozart parody, he adds two bars to the end, which does no harm. In the fughetta, Variation 24, the four entries of subject and answer do duty for Diabelli's tonic and dominant, and the rest of the pair of limericks evaporates into fugal ether. Variation 29, though in a slow tempo, compresses each part of the theme into six bars, of which the first four represent Diabelli's eight. Variation 30 is quite strict, but for the fact that, in representing Diabelli's upward step by the flat supertonic, Beethoven sends all the subsequent modulations to remoter regions. Instead of repeating either part, he elects to repeat the last four bars in the style of the French *petite reprise*, or refrain. Variation 31, being in enormously slow tempo, begins by quite adequately repeating each of Diabelli's four bars by one bar of 9/8, and then becomes rhapsodic on a much larger scale at the hint of Diabelli's rising sequence. The fugue merely takes a few notes from Diabelli's thrumming right hand as one fugue subject, and a vague hint of the rising sequences turned into falling sequences as the countersubject, or second subject. Perhaps, again, as in the fughetta, we may say that the scheme of a fugue exposition may do duty for Diabelli's tonic and dominant; but otherwise the point of this fugue is that it has definitely flown off at a tangent.

It is impossible to exaggerate the cogency and strictness of these variations—that is to say, the organic solidity of their relation to the theme. And this is a thing which the naïve listener is probably more capable of feeling than the listener who is brought up on such orthodox doctrines as lead people to accept without inquiry Mendelssohn's *Variations Sérieuses* as a classical example of variation form. It is true that neither Mendelssohn nor Schumann was able to see the sense in which Beethoven's variations are strict. Schumann probably thought that, where the original melody is not evident, Beethoven was indulging in a free episode; but, in his own case, Schumann felt uneasy enough about this to hesitate in the titles of his own variations. Hence, his *Impromptus*, op. 5, on a theme by Clara Wieck, which are very good variations indeed, resembling Beethoven's 'Prometheus' set in beginning with the bare bass; his *Études Symphoniques en forme de Variations*, which attempt half-heartedly and incorrectly to distinguish those études which are variations from those which are only études; and, lastly, the *Andante quasi variazioni* in the F major String Quartet, where the chief ground for Schumann's scruple is that he happens to have two themes instead of one. You cannot make a free episode into a variation by introducing a scrap of the original melody; and if your variation is true to your theme, you need not spoil it by any such apology for its lack of outward resemblance. The structure of true variations is aesthetically on much the same plan as a great painter's or sculptor's knowledge of anatomy. It is addressed to the eye, because the artist who has mastered his anatomy produces figures that look like living creatures, not like sacks or bladders stuffed or blown to the requisite size and approximate shape; but neither the artist nor the spectator has any use for an X-ray eye. The naïve listener will find in the momentum of Beethoven's and Brahms's variations all that he needs for their enjoyment. It is a matter of far less importance whether it takes him more or less time to see the inferiority of variations that are not on the true classical lines. There is no reason why he should be in a hurry to lose his capacity for enjoying lighter works, even though propaganda had been made for accepting them as a great advance upon the hidebound classics.

One thing, however, is really important, and that is to recognize that if a variation confines itself to embroidering the melody and does not, like some of the *Variations Sérieuses*, substitute weaker cadences for the originals, it cannot fail to maintain the momentum of the theme. Indeed, the essential cumulative effect of a set of variations can be maintained by sheer repetition without varying the theme at all. One of Beethoven's most impressive movements is the Allegretto which does duty for the slow movement in the Seventh Symphony; this is essentially a set of variations in which the sole means of variation consists in adding one counterpoint to the theme and repeating the combination in a crescendo up to the fortissimo of the full orchestra. After this, a new theme appears in the tonic major as a middle episode, or trio. Then we have another variation, in which the theme is in the bass and the counterpoint above it, followed by a very short fugal episode, which seems to intend to move off at a tangent; but at its first crescendo its energy fails, and one clause of the original theme, without its counterpoint, closes the matter, except for a final statement in which the whole theme dies away in antiphonal groups.

Not only are the sonata variations of Beethoven explicitly melodic, often of the lowest type, but their themes are, in an actual majority of cases, dependent on fine detail in the cadences, which simply will not bear any freedom in the variations. It is obvious that there is great danger in a criterion which, however correctly in point of science, describes as a low type of organization such sublime slow movements as those of the *Sonata Appassionata*, the B flat Trio, op. 97, the Violin Concerto, and the Ninth Symphony itself. The true criterion is perfectly accessible to the naïve listener. He will soon form a conception that does justice to these august occasions if he will think of the enormous responsibility of decorating a large space. We may pray for the artistic soul of the portrait-painter who is not yet so fashionable that he can afford to refuse to paint prosaic municipal authorities in their robes of office; but great painting has been shown in the apparently insolent few strokes that make the jewellery flash and give to the folds of the drapery a nobility which perhaps they cannot give to the wearer. Beethoven never accepted a commission that he disliked. He had good reason to be fond of his many friends among the Vienna aristocracy, and, if a pretty young Archduchess could walk across the floor with simple and royal dignity, there is no reason why an artist should not amuse himself and us by painting a series of portraits of her in various costumes. We do not as a rule go to Beethoven for such royal mannequin displays as the first movement of the A flat Sonata, op. 26, but we had much better go to Beethoven for them than to anybody else. There are, indeed, critics who tell us that Beethoven's ornamentation is bad, but they have never succeeded in giving us any criterion for what ornamentation is good; and if they tell us that this unsophisticated movement is no better than the effusions in a similar style by Hummel, Wölfl, and other pianoforte-writers, we may safely challenge them to produce examples which do not instantly show that Beethoven's is the real Princess.

A peculiarity of Beethoven's themes for sonata variations is very interesting, and I am not aware that it has been noticed elsewhere. It consists in a kind of finesse in all the cadences of the theme. We first find it in the very perfunctory set of variations in the G major Sonata, op. 14, no. 2. The first part of the theme reaches a dominant at the end of every second bar, and the four dominant cadences are accurately graded from the first half-close to the eventual full close in the key of the dominant. In the second part, we have a subdominant, very necessary to restore balance; but there still remain two dominant closes, one by way of preparation for reaffirming the tonic, and the other in the course of recapitulating the first half of the theme. Obviously, you cannot build upon this delicate structure any such variations as those on Diabelli's waltz.

Now turn to the exquisite variations in the A major Quartet, op. 18, no. 5. The ostentatious naïveté of the tonic and dominant base is in keeping with the wit of the melody, which goes down and up a hexachord with a nursery-rhyme kind of wit. Meanwhile, the viola has its own opinions, which it tells sleepily, like the tale of the Dormouse in the Hatter's tea-party in *Alice in Wonderland*. The second part begins by hovering around the tonic and subdominant, and ends with a final version of the scale-figure.

The variations in the *Sonata Appassionata* are *doubles* (that is to say, progressive subdivisions of the rhythmic units) on the boldest of all themes of this kind. All its cadences are tonic at every two bars, both in the first part and in the second, and the melody itself is, in its first part, as near monotony as possible. If the listener can see anything in the *Sonata Appassionata* at all, he cannot fail to understand that the point here is the contrast between the Nirvana-like inaction of the slow movement and the terrible tragedies that surround it. It is, in fact, a vision of a world away from action, and the most dramatic moment in the sonata is that in which the last variation substitutes an unexpected chord at the end. With this the vision is shattered, and all is overwhelmed in the torrential passion of the finale.

In other works, the Violin Concerto and the B flat Trio, op. 97, Beethoven uses variation form in order to express a sublime inaction in his slow movements. In the Violin Concerto, the theme is a single strain with an echo, and the inaction is the more impressive by reason of two episodic themes which intervene between the later variations, and which are even more confined to the home tonic than the theme itself. Vincent D'Indy, who had his own highly intellectual aesthetic philosophy, considered this not one of Beethoven's best movements, because its key-system is monotonous and its ornamentation exaggerated. The critic who finds the key-system monotonous cannot compel us to accept his judgement of ornamentation as final. We all have to learn by living, and even arbiters of taste are born, not made. In the long run, it will save time if we take Beethoven as an authority on ornamentation and consider it more probable that the fault is in us if we do not like the way in which he fills out a space. On paper, the very gorgeous ornamentation of the variations in the Trio, op. 97, may present the same appearance of blackness as a set of brilliant variations on 'Home Sweet Home' by a Victorian salon writer, but its quality is really quite different. No doubt it can be vulgarized by bad playing. Nothing is more false than the doctrine that great music cannot be ruined in performance. Not so long ago, a great impression was produced by a performance of *Hamlet* in modern costume. This was irreverently described as '*Hamlet* in plus-fours'. It had the paradoxical merit of bringing us back to the attitude of Elizabethan

audiences, who saw their Shakespeare acted in what was to them
ordinary modern costumes; but I do not think that *Hamlet* in
Cockney and Chicago dialects would have had any such effect.
If any one is under the delusion that such ornamentation as that
of the third variation in the Trio, op. 97, is easy to compose, or
much easier to play than to compose, I do not know how the
delusion is to be dispelled, for those who suffer from it will be
quite satisfied with their own attempts to parody such work.

In both the Violin Concerto and the B flat Trio, we encounter
drastic examples of Beethoven's disposition to shock his listeners
after he has deeply moved them. He used, we are told, to extemporize with such effect that his listeners were in tears, whereupon
he would burst into a loud guffaw and call them fools. Now this
may be impish, but it is not Mephistophelean. It is an outward
sign of one of the highest qualities of Beethoven's spiritual grace.
In a more conciliatory form, it is represented by William James's
profound observation that it is not good for us to be content to
enjoy art passively, and that, if we cannot ourselves be artists,
we must at all events not receive without giving; so that, for
instance, it would be a good thing for every non-musician who
has enjoyed a great musical experience to follow it by being kind
to his aunt or doing some similar act of disinterested duty. It is
a fundamental principle with Beethoven that not only tragedy and
comedy, but beatific visions and common daylight, are inextricably
mingled. We are told that, before he had left Bonn, he had
already formed the project of composing Schiller's 'Ode to Joy',
and the lines in that ode that most attracted him are those of the
Creator dwelling above the stars, and next, if not equal with these,
the strophe:

> 'Deine Zauber binden wieder,
> Was die Mode frech geteilt;
> Alle Menschen werden Brüder,
> Wo dein sanfter Flügel weilt'—

> 'Thy spells reunite what fashion had the effrontery to separate
> [Beethoven's autograph reads "frech" instead of "streng"
> *geteilt*]; all men become brothers under the shadow of thy
> kindly wings.'

This is the source of Beethoven's humour, and it is also the
reason why his pathos remains proof against all the effrontery of
fashion. If the present jumpings of the fashionable cat can achieve
anything but imbecility, we may anticipate this much real good
from a revived appreciation of Beethoven's humour; for while he
was incapable of irreverence, Johnson and Carlyle were not more
impatient of shams, and Shaw not more disposed than Beethoven

to laugh shams out of court. When the finale of the B flat Trio
shocks us with unseemly conviviality before the slow movement
has finished dying away, Beethoven has no apologies to offer.
The outrageous jocularity continues unabashed, until not only the
proportions, but the actual mysterious quality, of the finale
develop a sublimity of their own. Samuel Butler had an instinctive
reverence for Handel, and with the aid of a small talent for music,
a great talent for mimicry, and an unholy amount of hard work
at musical grammar, succeeded in producing quite amusing
imitations of Handel's choral writing; but Beethoven remained
a sealed book to him, and he ought to have put himself into one
of his own books as a comic character as a penance for his priggish-
ness at being scandalized by the theme of the rondo of Beethoven's
Violin Concerto. A critic who wishes the finale of that, or of any,
concerto to be as great or greater than the first movement is in
any case beyond redemption. Plato disposed of him once for all
under the figure of the artist who, arguing that purple is the most
beautiful of colours and the eye the most beautiful of human
features, proceeded to paint the eyes of all statues purple. A
music-lover will show himself to be a very ordinary person indeed
who fails to see that the rondo theme of the finale of Beethoven's
Violin Concerto is an extraordinary person and, as such, quite
a match for the other movements.

In his last works, Beethoven succeeded in writing codas to
slow sets of variations, so that the sublime inactivity could reveal
enough active energy to come to its own end, without being
interrupted by any commoner daylight. In two of the cases, there
is the delicate finesse with cadences which we already saw in
opus 14, no. 2. Both parts of the *Arietta* in the Sonata, op. 111,
are repeated, and the swing of tonic and dominant harmonies is
such that the first strain throws the harmonic emphasis on to the
dominant, and is thus complete, but on the repeat shifts the
balance so that it just becomes a tonic cadence. These details
are faithfully reproduced in the variations. In the E flat Quartet,
op. 127, the repeats are written out in full, because each of the
two strains is first given by the violin and answered by the violoncello, and also the half-close at the end of the first strain is on
repeat replaced by a full close in the dominant. To the second
strain a codetta is added on the repetition. The variations faithfully repeat these details, and the first and third variations even
reproduce the fact that the violin is answered by the violoncello.

The slow movement of the Ninth Symphony I have dealt with
in another connexion. The form has obviously gained great
energy from the presence of a second theme given twice in remote
keys. The subtle feature of the main theme consists in the echoes
which the wind instruments give to the phrases of the strings.

In the variations, these echoes remain almost unadorned, while the ornamentation of the strings increases.

In all these great sonata variations of Beethoven's last period, you will find the tendency of the coda to reassert the diurnal spin of the theme in final half-variations after the adventures of the coda.

Beethoven's last set of variations is the slow movement of the last String Quartet, op. 135. Here the theme consists of a single strain with echoes. The second variation is in the tonic minor, and takes advantage of the very clear and self-repeating structure of the theme by answering the first two bars in a foreign key, with the result that the following shorter sequences modulate more widely. It is to be hoped that the present comment leaves or restores to the listener enough naïveté to enable him to hear this movement as the perfectly straightforward set of variations which it happens to be. The last variation, like the minor variation, quits the melody of the theme, and can afford to do so, as there is no mistaking the very simple phrasing and harmonies. A slight expansion of the echoing cadences produces enough climax to end the movement almost in the ordinary course of the theme.

FUGUES

BEETHOVEN'S fugue-writing is a sore subject with many musicians. The popular and academic theory is that Beethoven could
not write fugues, that he notoriously had great difficulties with
his counterpoint when he was young, and not so very young
either, and that on the whole we may acquiesce in Albrechtsberger's
dictum that Beethoven knew nothing and would never carry out
anything in good style. The facts are not quite so simple. As
far as Beethoven is concerned, he was quite satisfied with his
capacity to write an ordinary academic fugue. At all events, he
remarked in later years that it was not at all difficult. As far as
fugue itself is concerned, we must honestly face the fact that the
rules of fugue as laid down in text-books have no classical founda-
tion at all. A recent writer has told us that Bach knew these
rules very well and broke them with impunity. But not only had
Bach never heard of them, but he himself drew up, in *Die Kunst
der Fuge*, a series of fugues with the avowed purpose of sys-
tematizing the art-form; and the writers of text-books, though
they quote examples from Bach, have never taken the slightest
notice of his classification. I do not know, and have little curiosity
to know, the historic origins of the academic fugue form as
commonly taught. I see traces of it in Haydn's fugues and in
Beethoven's—that is to say, I can see that the device of causing
the subject and answer to overlap in stretto is regarded by these
masters as a special effect of climax, and is in Haydn's case marked
off from the earlier stages of a fugue by a rhetorical pause. . . .

INDEX

of Musical Works mentioned in the Text